Jerome D. Davis

**A Maker of New Japan Rev. Joseph Hardy Neesima, LL.D**

president of Doshisha university, Kyoto

Jerome D. Davis

**A Maker of New Japan Rev. Joseph Hardy Neesima, LL.D**
*president of Doshisha university, Kyoto*

ISBN/EAN: 9783337170387

Printed in Europe, USA, Canada, Australia, Japan

Cover: Foto ©Lupo / pixelio.de

More available books at **www.hansebooks.com**

# A MAKER OF NEW JAPAN

## Rev. JOSEPH HARDY NEESIMA
LL.D.

PRESIDENT OF DOSHISHA UNIVERSITY, KYOTO

BY

REV. J. D. DAVIS, D. D.

PROFESSOR OF THEOLOGY IN DOSHISHA UNIVERSITY

✝

"*For me to live is Christ, to die is gain*"
PHIL. i, 21
"*For none of us liveth to himself, and none dieth to himself*"
ROM. xiv, 7

*With many Illustrations*

FLEMING H. REVELL COMPANY
NEW YORK    CHICAGO    TORONTO
*Publishers of Evangelical Literature*

# PREFACE TO THE FIRST EDITION

THE life, character, and work of our brother who was so recently "called up higher" were remarkable and unique; much of his life was spent in our midst here in Kyoto. For over fourteen years it was my privilege to be very intimately associated with him, and I have been asked to prepare a brief sketch of his life which may perhaps serve as an introduction to larger works which will doubtless be published later both in Japan and in the United States.

In preparing this sketch I have consulted Dr. Neesima's diary, written before he left his home for Hakodate, while on the voyage thither, and in Hakodate, up to the day he sailed from that place on his great quest for truth, and also a copy of the brief sketch of his life written by the late Miss Phebe Fuller McKeen, one of his Sabbath-school teachers; this sketch was written after Dr. Neesima had been in Phillips Academy, Andover, Mass., about a year. I have quoted freely from the latter in the first chapter and the beginning of the second, using Dr. Neesima's own words in broken English which he wrote out, or which his teacher above referred to copied from his lips before he had had an opportunity to master the English language. I have also quoted from his journal written on his trip around the world in 1884–85; I also quote freely from letters received from our brother during the last fifteen years, and I give in some detail the history of the founding of the Doshisha schools, the great work of Dr. Neesima's life.

His presence with us has been a blessing, and his memory is a benediction to us all. My hope and prayer is that God may use this sketch for his own glory in the advancement of his Kingdom in Japan.

J. D. DAVIS.

DOSHISHA, KYOTO, February, 1890.

# Preface to the Third Edition

THE ten years which have elapsed since the first American edition appeared have been eventful ones in Japan and in the institution to which Dr. Neesima gave his life.

The nationalistic and materialistic waves which were rising ten years ago, and which, for a time, threatened to change the character and the fundamental Christian principles of the Constitution of Doshisha, have spent their force, and the school is established on a permanent basis, in accordance with the new Civil Code of Japan. The new Board of Directors, five years ago, unanimously adopted a resolution stating that: "While it is invested with the title to the property of the institution and charged with its management, it holds all the properties of the Company in trust to carry out the wishes and purposes of its founder, in accordance with the unchangeable provisions of the Constitution." The members of the Board also stated that their understanding of the Christianity "which is to form the basis of the moral teaching in all the departments of the Doshisha school, under the unchangeable principles of the Constitution, is that body of living and fundamental Christian principles believed and accepted by the great Christian Churches of the world."

Nearly five hundred and fifty students were enrolled in the school during the last school year, and its Christian spirit, its discipline and its *esprit de corps* are constantly improving. The school is loyal to the memory and the principles of its founder.

A glance, taken a year ago, at the outcome of the school shows that it has had, and is having no small part in the moulding and regeneration of this nation, which is astonishing the world by her progress along all material lines of advancement, and especially by her success in the mighty struggle in which she is now engaged with Russia. More than five thousand students have entered the school since its beginning. Of these, nearly one thousand have been graduated. In March, 1903, it was found that, of these graduates, over eighty were preaching the Gospel, one hundred and sixty-one were teaching, two hundred and twenty-one were engaged in business, one hundred and fifty-six were studying, twenty-seven were officials, sixteen were editors, etc.

Over one hundred graduates of the Girls' Department were in homes of their own, most of them centres of Christian homes, while more than seventy graduates of the Training School for Nurses were engaged as nurses.

About four thousand have left the school before graduation, and very many of these are engaged in useful work as preachers, teachers, etc.

The school looks forward into the future with great hope and courage. The rapidly increasing Christian constituency of the school, and the fact that the higher schools in Japan cannot receive more than one-third of the graduates of the Government Middle Schools, open a great field for the Doshisha, for it can furnish courses of study for young men to fit them for practical work along the lines which are most needed now in Japan, and at the same time give them the Christian teaching and the moral influence they need to make them men of character and ability.

The school greatly needs a larger endowment. It is crippled for lack of funds to do the work which is opening before it. May the time be hastened when some of those who are able to endow the educational institutions of America with their millions, shall have their vision and their love so broadened that they will gladly give to such institutions as Doshisha, in Japan and in China, their much needed endowment!

With many hundreds of Chinese and Corean young men and

young women sent to Japan for education, with China and Corea looking to Japan to guide and help them up to civilization, to say nothing of the needs of the forty-five millions of the Japanese people, before us, is there any place in the wide world where money used to endow and equip such a school as the Doshisha will bring a larger return for time and for eternity, for the money invested ?

It would seem to be due to the memory of the noble soul who devoted his life to the founding of this institution that it should be helped in this substantial way and thus realize Dr. Neesima's hopes for it, and shine with an ever-increasing lustre like that which surrounds the name of its lamented founder.

J. D. DAVIS.

*January, 1905.*

# CONTENTS

CHAPTER I.
BIRTH, EARLY EDUCATION, AND START FROM JAPAN......... 15

CHAPTER II.
TRIALS AND PREPARATION ............................... 29

CHAPTER III.
LAYING FOUNDATIONS...................................... 47

CHAPTER IV.
MARRIAGE, TRIALS, AND WORK ........................... 61

CHAPTER V.
BROADENING PLANS, TOUR ABROAD ........................ 85

CHAPTER VI.
LAST DAYS, DEATH, AND BURIAL ......................... 109

CHAPTER VII.
TRIBUTES AND LESSONS................................... 119

# LIST OF ILLUSTRATIONS

| | | |
|---|---|---|
| JOSEPH HARDY NEESIMA AND HIS WIFE ............... | *Frontispiece* | |
| THE SACRED MOUNTAIN .......................... | *Facing page* | 16 |
| NEESIMA IN HAKODATE, 1864 ......................... | " | 22 |
| NEESIMA DRESSED AS A SERVANT ..................... | " | 24 |
| HON. ALPHEUS HARDY ............................... | " | 32 |
| NEESIMA'S WIFE AND MOTHER ....................... | " | 62 |
| FIRST THEOLOGICAL HALL, DOSHISHA UNIVERSITY ..... | " | 67 |
| RECITATION HALL, DOSHISHA UNIVERSITY ............. | " | 74 |
| LIBRARY HALL, DOSHISHA UNIVERSITY ................ | " | 86 |
| SCIENCE HALL, DOSHISHA UNIVERSITY ................. | " | 92 |
| CLARK THEOLOGICAL HALL, DOSHISHA UNIVERSITY ..... | " | 100 |
| NEW CHAPEL ........................................ | " | 110 |
| NEESIMA'S RESIDENCE ............................... | " | 124 |
| NEESIMA'S STUDY .................................... | " | 136 |
| FIRST CLASS IN DOSHISHA ............................ | " | 148 |
| LAST RESTING-PLACE ................................ | " | 154 |

Neesima's Coat of Arms.

# I
# BIRTH, EARLY EDUCATION, AND START FROM JAPAN

"*Now the Lord said unto Abram, Get thee out of thy country, and from thy kindred, and from thy father's house, unto the land that I will show thee.*"—GENESIS XII. 1.

> " God moves in a mysterious way
> His wonders to perform."
> COWPER.

> "*Faith is nothing else but the soul's venture.*"
> W. BRIDGE.

> " Rashly,
> And praised be rashness for it—let us know,
> Our indiscretion sometimes serves us well,
> When our deep plots do pall; and that should teach us,
> There's a divinity that shapes our ends,
> Rough-hew them how we will."
> SHAKESPEARE.

## CHAPTER I

BIRTH, EARLY EDUCATION, AND START FROM JAPAN

THE long sleep of the island empire was broken. The fleet of "barbarian" ships which cast anchor in the Bay of Yedo on that Sabbath morning, July 7, 1853, under command of Commodore Perry, finally caused the nation which had been closed for two hundred and fifty years to open its gates to the world. There followed a development along lines of material progress more rapid than the world had ever before witnessed. Japan sent her keenest statesmen to search through the enlightened nations of the world for the best they could find, and tried to advance as far in thirty years as the nations of the West had done in as many decades. God touched the heart of one young man among the many thousands in the Eastern capital, and fitted him to bear a conspicuous part in that moral revolution which is needed as the counterpart of the external revolution, and without which the rapid material progress cannot be lasting.

Mr. Neesima was born in Yedo, January 14, 1843, Japanese old style. According to the Western mode of reckoning it was February 12, 1843. He was a samurai, one of the retainers of a daimio of the province of Kodzuke, the castle town of which was Annaka, about seventy miles from Tokyo. He was born in Tokyo, in the house of Itakura, a prince of this province. His father (Neesima

Tamaharu) was writing-master of the prince's house, and served also as steward, having charge of the private servants and attendants of the prince.

The family consisted, besides himself, of a younger brother, who died while he was in America, and four sisters, only one of whom survives. Mr. Neesima's father died in 1886, but his mother still survives (1894), at the advanced age of eighty-eight years.

In later years he wrote as follows of his mother: "She was a very kind-hearted woman, always ready to assist her neighbors, although she found so much to do in her own family. One day she was sick in bed; I was very anxious for her, and wished to procure some remedy, though she had something from the doctor. So I went to the temple and prayed to the god that he would cure my mother; I bought a little bit of cake, which was a portion of the morning offering, and gave it to her for a remedy, hoping earnestly that it might do some good to her. I knew not, indeed, whether nature cured her, or whether her will or faith in the god made her whole, but she became better soon after she received that cake. She truly believed that the god had granted my earnest request for her, and restored her health so soon. I had done the same thing for my neighbors, and was often successful in curing them."

The above extract and the one which follows show the religious nature of the boy, and his faithfulness, although he early learned to distrust the gods of his fathers. "I was obedient to my parents, and, as they early taught me to do, served gods made by hand with great reverence. I strictly observed the days of my ancestors and departed friends, and we went to the graveyards to worship their spirits. I often rose up early in the morning, went to a temple which was at least three and a half miles from home,

THE SACRED MOUNTAIN

## Birth, Early Education, and Start from Japan 17

where I worshiped the gods, and returned promptly, reaching home before breakfast. I did that not only because I expected some blessing from the gods, but that I might receive praise from my parents and neighbors."

The coming of Commodore Perry when he was ten years old quite stirred young Neesima's heart. Of this he wrote: "Although I was then quite young, yet I desired to be a brave soldier or a man of honor, like those whom I found so often in our ancient history. I frequently went to the temple of the god of war, prayed sincerely that he would give me strength, and often performed very foolish ceremonies for his service. Once, when I was reading a life of a Chinese hero, I came across a famous phrase which he proclaimed when he quitted the sword-exercise: 'A sword is only designed to slay a single man, but I am going to learn to kill ten thousand enemies.' That is, he was inclined to study some work of strategy. Though I was not able to measure my own quality, yet I desired to follow his example, and wished to kill many thousands of enemies, not by a sword, but by strategy. This thought helped me to quit sword-exercise and to confine myself entirely to study. I studied very diligently, and *often went to bed after cock-crow.*"

The quotations in the sketch which follows on the next few pages were written in imperfect English before he had been in America a year, and are taken from "The Story of Neesima," written by Miss Phebe F. McKeen. About the time he was sixteen years old he was engaging in the study of the Chinese language with great enthusiasm when his prince "picked up me to write his daily book; although it would not had been my desire, I was obliged to go up his office." A new light dawned upon him about this time. "A day my comrade sent me a Atlas of United States, which was written in Chinese letter by some

American minister. I read it many times, and I was wondered so much as my brain would melted out of my head, because I liked it very much; picking one president, building free schools, poor-houses, house of correction, and machine-working, and so forth, and I thought that a government of every country must be as President of United States. And I murmured myself that, O governor of Japan! why you keep down us, as a dog or a pig? We are people of Japan; if you govern us, you must love us as your children. From that time I wished to learn American knowledge, but, alas! I could not got any teacher to learn it. Although I would not like to learn Holland, I was obliged to learn it, because so many of my countrymen understood to read it."

But it was difficult for him to find time for the study of Dutch. Once when his prince had, for the second time, caught him running away from the office to go to his Dutch teacher, and had given him a flogging for it, he asked: "'Why you run out from here?' Then I answered him that 'I wish to learn foreign knowledge, because foreigners have got best knowledge, and I hope to understand very quickly; therefore, though I know I must stay here and reverence your law, my soul went to my master's house to learn it, and my body was obliged to go thither too.' Then he said to me very kindly, 'You can write Japan very well, and you can learn yourself enough with it; if you don't run away from here any more, I will give you more wages. With what reason will you like foreign knowledge? Perhaps it will mistake yourself.' I said to him sooner, 'Why will it mistake myself? I guess every one must take some knowledge. If a man has not any knowledge, I will worth him as a dog or a pig.' Then he laughed and said me, 'You are a stable boy.'"

This was not the only time that thirst for knowledge

brought him both ridicule and blows. His family and acquaintances thought him very foolish to be craving needless knowledge, still he "never took care to them," and "held his stableness very fast." His work increased, however, so that he had no time for study, and this cost him "many musings in my head"; and at last he became fairly sick with thwarted purposes and unsatisfied longings. After various efforts to cure him, his physician told him, "Your sickness comes from your mind; you must try to destroy your warm mind, and must take walk for the healthfulness of your body, and it would be more better than many medicine." "My prince gave me plenty times to feed my weakness, and my father gave me some money to play myself;" all of which he devoted to the study of Dutch. "A small 'Book of Nature,' which fell into his hands, delighted him so much that it proved "more better to my sickness than doctor's medicines."

So health came back, and with it came the busy days and studious nights. In his "Book of Nature" he met with some things he was unable to understand, because he had never studied arithmetic; so he went to an arithmetic school until he had mastered enough to go through his "Book of Nature" intelligently. Here are some reflections of this young seeker after knowledge in his own words: "Some day I went to the seaside of Yedo, hoping to see the view of the sea. I saw largest man-of-war of Dutch lying there, and she seemed to me as a castle or as a battery, and I thought, too, that she would be strong enough to fight with enemy. While I look upon her, one reflection came upon my head, that we must open navy, because my country is surrounded by water, and if foreigners fight to my country, we must fight with them at sea. But I made other reflection, too: that, since foreigners trade, price of everything get high, the country get poor; therefore, because the countrymen don't understand to do trade with foreigners, therefore we must know to do trade, and we must learn foreign knowledge. But the government's law neglected all my thoughts, and I cried out myself, Why government? why not let us be free? why let us be as a bird in a cage or as a rat in a bag?"

So he set to work in a government marine school whenever he could get away from his work, seeking information which he might turn to account for his country in the future. He had just made a good beginning in navigation when night study injured his eyes so that he was obliged to leave books entirely for a year and a half, "which would not come again in my life." He had hardly recovered from this trouble so as to resume his place in his prince's office when he was beset with measles, and his eyes, in consequence, "began to spoil again," so that he was obliged to "spend many times very vainly." When he did begin to use his eyes again, however, it was to some purpose. "A day I visited my friend, and I found out small Holy Bible in his library, that was written by some American minister in China language and had shown only the most remarkable events of it. I lend it from him and read it at night. I was afraid the savage country's law, which if I read the Bible will cross," i.e., crucify, "my whole family."

This abridgement of the Bible contained little but the grand facts of creation and redemption, and these were entirely new to this earnest young soul who pored over its pages. The opening sentence of this book was: "In the beginning God created the heavens and the earth." He says: "I put down the book and look around me, saying, Who made me? my parents? No, my God. God made my parents and let them make me. Who made my table? a carpenter? No, my God. God let trees grow upon the earth; although a carpenter made up this table, it indeed came from trees; then I must be thankful to God, I must believe him, and I must be upright against him." He at once recognized his Maker's claim to love and obedience, and began to yield them; he prayed, "Oh, if you have eyes, look upon me; if you have ears, listen for me." It was a long time after this, however, that he first learned to pray as a man talketh with his friend.

From this time his "mind was fulfilled to read English Bible," and he "burned to find some teacher or missionary" who could teach him.

His father was disturbed by his boy's new notions, and certain that he would get the whole family into trouble; and on asking permission of his prince and his parents to go to Hakodate, where he hoped to meet some Englishman or American, he got not only a refusal, but a flogging. Still "my stableness did not destroy by their expostulations." He next applied to a relative of his prince, a noble higher in authority and rank than he, and got leave from him to go in one of his vessels to Hakodate. Now he had gained his point, neither his father nor his prince could prevent him.

This was in March, 1864, and when he heard this news he exclaimed, "Oh, heaven does not cast me off; the great point of my business is in this one thing," and he leaped for joy. He went to his room, packed such of his belongings as he desired to take with him, but he could not sleep at all till morning; and on March 11th (O. S.), with great pain, but with a resolute heart, he left his family in tears and started on his search for truth, "not thinking that when money was gone, how would I eat and dress myself, but only casting myself on the providence of God."

On the 13th the ship sailed away from the harbor, and he was on the great ocean. He had told his mother that he would be gone a year, he thought, but he little suspected then that it would be more than ten years before he would again see his native city, and look into the faces of those he loved. His diary for the next seven weeks is intensely interesting. The sailing-junk in which he went stopped at many of the principal towns along the coast, as Uraga, Sendai, Kumagasaki, etc., to survey the harbors or to escape storms. Our young voyager was now twenty-one years old, and he made good use of his time in seeking for all the information possible about each of these places. His diary contains a minute description of each one of them, a map of the harbor, the governor's name, the number of counties into which the province is divided, and, if a castle town, the condition of the castle, and the history of the province; also the size of the town, its taxes, whether light or heavy, the productions of the place, what kinds of woods are produced, what kinds of fish are exported, etc.

He is surprised at the great abundance of the rice-whisky, or sake, which was retailed at three cents a quart. There was one other item which he recorded in this diary concerning these places which I wish those foreigners who, after a brief residence in Japan, go home and report that its morality is superior to that of Christian lands, could read or see for themselves. His picture of the number of prostitutes in these trading-towns is a fearful one, too fearful, some of it, to reproduce here. In one of these towns he says there were from two to four of these women in each house in the town; he was greatly astonished and shocked at it himself, although he freely indulged in sake-drinking with his comrades while in these harbors.

April 21st (O. S.) he reached Hakodate, then an open port, with English, American, and Russian consulates in it. Young Neesima was, however, doomed to disappointment at first, as he sought in vain for any teacher of English; and his small funds melted away very fast, and he was obliged to look about him for means to feed the outer man as well as the inner. In this he was successful, as he fell in with Père Nikolai, the Russian priest who has since so successfully taught the religion of the Greek Church in Japan. Nikolai was glad to secure his services as a teacher of Japanese, so he removed to Nikolai's house and began his work.

He found a few wide-awake young Japanese among the acquaintances he made, and among them Mr. Munokite, a clerk in an English store, who could speak English tolerably well, and who played a most important part in the next great act in the drama of Neesima's life. Meeting with these young friends from time to time, he told them of his intense desire to learn foreign knowledge, and they encouraged him. But on account of the great difficulties connected with learning it in Japan, he conceived the idea of leaving the country altogether. The more he saw of his native land the more he longed to be able to "bring a light into the darkness"; but it was a very serious question. If he left the country death would be his only welcome back. To go was to adventure himself, a penniless wanderer with an unknown tongue, into a vast, mysterious world of which he only knew that truth was there. Worst of all, it would bring grief and fear, possibly danger and death, into the home he loved. He spent much time in thinking over this momentous question; he discharged his duty as a teacher to Père Nikolai faithfully, and as his employer went every day to the Russian hospital to have his eyes treated, young Neesima went with him, and in his diary he describes in minute detail all the appointments of this hospital, its buildings, its beds, its diet, its medicines, and most of all, the fact that the poor were treated without money and without price. All this made a deep impression upon his mind; and the more he studied over the great question the more he felt impelled to leave his country. He even gradually found reasons to justify him in going, notwithstanding the strong filial ties which bound him to his parents and friends. He says: "One reflection came upon my head, that, although my parents made and fed me, I belong indeed to Heavenly Father; therefore I must believe him and I must run in his way; then I began to search some vessel to get out from the country."

If every soul was as loyal to truth as was this one, as earnestly seeking it, as loyally obeying and following it, this world would soon become the very gate of heaven. His young English-speaking friend finally secured for him a passage in an American schooner, the "Berlin," Captain Savory, bound for Shanghai. It was necessary to get away with the utmost secrecy. He made all his arrangements, picked out a small bundle of his clothes which he could carry on his back; he had a letter written, purporting to come from his brother in Tokyo, saying that his father was very sick, and that he must hurry home. Providentially, Père Nikolai had gone away out of town, but he showed the letter to his servants and to some others, and removed all his goods to a friend's house. Toward evening he took his little bundle of clothes and met his three friends for the last time. They had a supper together, and passed around the sake-cup in token of friendship. Neesima wrote a short poem, all wished him well, expressed a desire to accompany him, and bade him goodby. About midnight our young hero, dressed as a servant, with his bundle on his back, sallied out into the darkness, following one of his friends, who was dressed as a samurai, with his two swords in plain sight. They wended their

NEESIMA DRESSED AS A SERVANT

way by back streets down to the water's edge, where his friends had a small boat waiting for him; he was placed in the bottom of the boat and covered up, with orders to appear as a woman who was being taken out to the ship, if they were hailed. A whispered word of parting, hushed footsteps, the muffled dip of an oar, and the true-hearted young patriot who went to seek light and blessing for his country had stolen away from her shores like a culprit, and was soon on board the American schooner, the date of his embarkation being July 18, 1864.

# II
## TRIALS AND PREPARATION

*" Wherein ye greatly rejoice, though now for a little while, if need be, ye have been put to grief in manifold temptations, that the proof of your faith, being more precious than gold that perisheth though it is proved by fire, might be found unto praise and glory and honor at the revelation of Jesus Christ."*—1 PET. I. 6, 7.

> " A raveled rainbow overhead
> Lets down to life its varying thread—
> Love's blue, joy's gold, and, fair between,
> Hope's shifting light of emerald-green;
> While either side, in deep relief,
> A crimson pain, a violet grief!
> Wouldst thou amid their gleaming hues
> Clutch after those and these refuse?
> Believe! as thy beseeching eyes
> Follow their lines and sound the skies,
> There, where the fadeless glories shine,
> An unseen angel twists the twine;
> And be thou sure, what tint soe'er
> The sunbeam's broken rays may wear,
> It needs them all, that, broad and white,
> God's love may weave the perfect light."
>
> MRS. A. D. T. WHITNEY.

> " Through black waves and stormy blast,
> And out of the fog-wreath dense and dun,
> Guided and held shall the vessel run,
> Gain the fair haven, night being past,
> And anchor in the sun."
>
> SUSAN COOLIDGE.

## CHAPTER II

### TRIALS AND PREPARATION

OUR young friend was cordially received on board the schooner by the kind-hearted captain, but he could not sleep any that night, and in the early morning Japanese officials were seen coming to search the ship, to make sure that no Japanese was secreted on board. The captain hid Mr. Neesima in his own private room and locked the door. The search was completed, but our hero was not discovered, and the ship weighed anchor, spread her sails, and moved out to sea.

And now our young exile began to think what he had done. He had written a long letter to his prince, telling him of his decision; he had written another to his home friends, urging them not to mourn; but as he passed out to sea, and saw the mountains of his native land fade from his vision and disappear, very sad thoughts filled his heart. To add to his anguish, he was expected to do servile work on the ship, and as he had never done any such work, his samurai blood rebelled. Once or twice, when he was rudely ordered by the sailors to perform some menial task, he thought of seizing his sword and cutting down the men who seemed to be insulting him; but as he reflected that he could not thus realize his great purpose, he calmed his passions and meekly submitted to the indignity. Again, he had less than four dollars in money when he came on board, and this ship would only go as far as Shanghai. What should he do then?

He had a very disagreeable passage to Shanghai, and he was there for ten days in great doubt and fear lest he should be betrayed and taken back to Japan; but finally he had the joy of finding an American vessel, the "Wild Rover," bound for Boston. By much effort he succeeded in making the captain understand that he would be glad to do anything, and ask no other pay than to be taken to America. His own words are: "I begged him, if I get to America, please let me go to a school, and take good education." So the captain took him as his own servant, dressed him in foreign costume, gave him the name Jo, and on the voyage taught him navigation and English.

The voyage was long and tedious. The "Wild Rover" sailed along the coast of China to Manila and Saigon, trading here and there for eight months, before turning toward home. While they lay in the harbor of Hong Kong, Mr. Neesima found a New Testament in Chinese; he felt that he must have it, but how should he get it, since he had promised to ask the captain for no money? He thought of his sword, and he finally sold it and bought the New Testament.

At last sails were set for the West, and in four months from that time the land of promise dawned upon our wanderer.

During his life of a year on the "Wild Rover," as Mr. Neesima told the writer, he began to read his New Testament in the Chinese language. He could only spell out the meaning, but he began at Matthew and read on in course through Matthew, Mark, and Luke, and in the midst of the voyage he came to the sixteenth verse of the third chapter of John: "God so loved the world, that he gave his only begotten Son, that whosoever believeth on him shall not perish, but have everlasting life," and this made a very deep impression upon him, and he felt that this was just such a Saviour as he needed.

His faith and patience were sorely tried on the long voyage, and when he reached the harbor of Boston it seemed to him as if he were to be baffled. Directly after coming into port at Boston, the captain hurried away to see his friends, and for ten weeks young Neesima was left, "with rough and godless men who kept the ship," doing hard, heavy work, such as he had never been accustomed to. Besides this, everybody he met on the wharf frightened him; they told him: "Nobody on shore will relieve you, because since the war the price of everything got high; ah, you must go to sea again." "I thought, too," he says, "that I must work pretty well for my eating and dressing, and I could not get in any schools before I could earn money to pay to a school. When such thoughts pressed my brain I could not work very well; I could not read book very cheerfully, and I only looked around myself a long time as a lunatic."

He made one great discovery, however, during this tedious waiting-time. The captain had given him a little money to amuse himself with on shore, and he had bought a copy of "Robinson Crusoe," which he found in a second-hand book-store on Washington Street, and "Robinson Crusoe" first taught him that he might pray to his Heavenly Father as to a present, personal friend; and so every night, after he went to bed, he "prayed to the God, Please don't cast me away into miserable condition. Please let me reach my great aim."

How little we know when we pray how long our Heavenly Father has been preparing to answer our prayers! What comfort there is in the thought that both we and our prayers, our needs and their answers, were all present with God when he made his plan, and that he has been preparing from all eternity to answer our prayers in the best way.

The God who had turned this boy's heart away from idols; who had inspired him to "feel after him, if haply he might find him"; who had said to him, "Get thee out of thy country, and from thy kindred, and from thy father's house, unto the land that I will show thee"—this same God had not neglected to prepare a place for him in the land of promise to which he had led him. He had brought the young wanderer across the seas in a ship belonging to one of his own children, straight to the hands of one whose joy it was to spend his strength and his wealth in the service of his Master.

When the owner of the ship, the Hon. Alpheus Hardy, was finally told, by the captain, of this bright young Japanese who had thus come in search of truth, he at once declared that he would provide some way for his support. "When I first heard these things from my captain," said Mr. Neesima, "I jumped for joy; my eyes was fulfilled with many tears, because I was very thankful to him, and thought, 'God will not forsake me.'" Mr. Hardy met the young Japanese later, and asked him what his name was. "The sailors called me Jo," was the reply. "You are well named," said Mr. Hardy; "God has sent you to be a savior to your people." His benefactor little knew, when he spoke those words, how much of truth there was in them.

Mr. Hardy's first thought was to employ him as a house servant, but he soon found that he was not fitted for this; and in the meantime Mrs. Hardy had asked him to write out the reasons why he had left his native land and come to America. He did so in his broken English, and when Mr. and Mrs. Hardy read his story they felt that God had

HON. ALPHEUS HARDY

sent him, and they accepted the sacred trust, and decided to give him a thorough education.

The following is perhaps the first account which has ever been published of the struggle through which this benefactor of Mr. Neesima passed when he was obliged to give up his early life-purpose to become a minister. It was written by one who heard the speech of Mr. Hardy, and was published in the August number of the *North Wisconsin Evangel* for 1893, and quoted in the *Congregationalist* for August 31, 1893.

"This friend of Joseph Neesima and princely benefactor of countless good causes told once the following thrilling story to the Psi Upsilon Society at Amherst College, of which he had just been made an honorary member:

"I am not a college man, and it was the bitter disappointment of my life that I could not be one. I wanted to go to college and become a minister; went to Phillips Academy to fit. My health broke down, and in spite of my determined hope of being able to go on, at last the truth was forced on me that I could not. To tell my disappointment is impossible. It seemed as if all my hope and purpose and interest in life were defeated. 'I cannot be God's minister,' was the sentence that kept rolling through my mind. When that fact at last became certain to me, one evening alone in my room, my distress was so great that I threw myself flat on the floor. The voiceless cry of my soul was, 'O God, I cannot be thy minister.' Then there came to me as I lay a vision, a new hope, a perception that I could serve God in business with the same devotion as in preaching, and that to make money for God might be my sacred calling. The vision of this service, and its nature as a sacred ministry, were so clear and joyous that I rose to my feet and with new hope in my heart exclaimed aloud, 'O God, I *can* be thy minister! I will go back to Boston. I will make money for God, and *that* shall be my ministry. From that time,' continued Mr. Hardy, 'I have felt myself to be as much appointed and ordained to make money for God as if I had been permitted to carry out my own plan and been ordained to preach the Gospel. I am God's man, and the ministry to which God has called me is to make and administer money for him, and I consider myself responsible to discharge this ministry and to give account of it to him.'"

Mr. Hardy placed young Neesima in Phillips Academy at Andover, where he made the best use of his opportunities, and where for the first time he fully realized his sins and publicly accepted Christ as his Saviour, uniting with the church of Christ. Who can doubt, however, that he was accepted of God before this, and that he would have been ready to gladly bow before his Saviour and worship him if he had died in the midst of his long voyage in search of truth?

The following letter was written by Mr. Neesima, when he had been in America less than a year, to the Japanese friend who helped him get away from Hakodate.

"ANDOVER, February 23, 1866.
"*Mr. Munokite,*
"DEAR SIR:
"I am very well through God's mercy. Since I commenced my hazardous adventure I have spent many valuable days in hard work; oh! sometimes I had very miserable work: but this work I did not do for money, but for true knowledge. When I called on Him who made heaven and earth and sea, and all that in them is, my sorrow turned into joy, and my misery to success. Oh, I may surely say it is very wonderful and marvelous that such success has fallen on me! I passed through many thousand miles of water very safely without hurricane, tempest, or any trouble. When I came to Boston, the ship's owner, Mr. Alpheus Hardy, and the ship's captain, Horace S. Taylor, relieved me from my miserable condition, and gave me all things which I needed, and sent me to the academy at Andover, Mass., to get an education, paying my board and all expenses.

"I came to the house of Mr. Hidden—he don't keep any boarder but me only—and he and his sister care for me as much as for one of their own family, and I am very much enjoyed to stay here. Also I find a kind and religious man in Mr. Flint, a neighbor who was a teacher of some higher school for thirteen years. Every evening he hears me recite in arithmetic, that is named Eaton's Higher School Arithmetic, and his wife explains to me the most holy and valuable book in the world, entitled the New Testament, and tells about our Saviour, Jesus Christ, who was sent down from his Father to enlighten the darkness and save sinners. In the academy I am studying reading, spelling, grammar, and the same arithmetic; also I have a Bible-lesson every Sabbath. All the teachers and scholars, and many who know about me, are interested in me and love me, and some give me things to please me. But these things they don't do for my sake, but for the Lord Jesus Christ.

"Oh, dear friend, think you well who is Christ. The same is the Light which shines on the benighted and wicked world and guides us unto the way of salvation. The light of candle is blown away, but this is the true light of eternal life, and we can by no wise blow it out, and we may take this life through Jesus Christ. 'For God so loved the world, that he gave his only begotten Son, that whosoever believeth on him should not perish, but have everlasting life. For God sent not his Son into the world to condemn the world, but that the world through him might believe.'

"Oh, dear friend, I have nothing to repay your kindness, but will send only, study the Bible, and my photograph. Please care for your health, and study the book I have mentioned above. Oh, alas! it is not the country's law to study the Bible and worship our tender and merciful

Father who made us, loved us, and gave his only begotten Son, through whom we may be saved. But the law ought to be broken, because it is made by the devil, the king of the world. The world was not made by the devil, but by our true Father, who gave unto us his true law. O friend, whether then is right in the sight of God to hearken unto the devil more than unto God, please judge you.

"If the fierce devil persecute you for righteousness' sake, don't trouble yourself; I am sure God will protect you from all evil, and though your body should be killed, your soul would be received unto him, and you would dwell in the brightest place with eternal life. I would like, indeed, to go there with you.

"Your truly friend,
"NEESIMA SIMATA."

In due time he was ready for college, and entered Amherst College, where he was graduated in 1870. The statement of President Seelye, when asked for testimonials for Mr. Neesima, as he was about to return to Japan, will be a sufficient comment upon his faithfulness in college. Said the president: "*You cannot gild gold.*"

His faithfulness and thoroughness as a student are shown by the fact that he had in his possession a pile of large books nearly two feet high, which are filled with lectures and notes which he copied or wrote out while he was in college and in the theological seminary.

He entered Andover Theological Seminary, and in the fall of 1871, when I was in attendance at the meeting of the American Board at Salem, Mass., just before I sailed to Japan, Mr. Neesima elbowed his way through the great crowd and found me; and when I answered his eager question by stating that I was going to Japan, he seized my hand, and with tears in his eyes, told me how glad he was to meet me, and he wished me a hearty God-speed, and said he hoped to go back too before long.

In the winter of 1871-72 the second Japanese embassy, consisting of Messrs. Iwakura, Okubo, Kido, Ito, Terashima, and Tanaka, crossed the Pacific, and, after being snow-bound for a week at Salt Lake City, finally reached Washington. The embassy at once felt the need of some one to act as interpreter who could also help them in their examination of the institutions of these foreign lands, especially educational. Hearing of Mr. Neesima, who had then been in America about seven years, they sent him an invitation to come and meet them in Washington. Then the question of how to meet them arose in Mr. Neesima's mind. It had been the custom in Japan from time immemorial for a man to bow to the earth when meeting a superior, prostrating himself before him. Mr. Neesima finally decided to meet them in the American way, and went on to Washington. He was most cordially received by Mr. Mori, the Japanese minister at Washington. Twelve Japanese students, who were being supported in the United States by the Japanese government, had been summoned at the same time to meet the Japanese commissioner of education. They all met in one of the parlors of the Arlington House. The following are extracts from Mr. Neesima's letters written at this time.

"Mr. Mori said to the commissioner of education: 'Mr. Neesima came here at my request, not as a bondman, but with his kindness to give you some advice concerning education; so you must appreciate his kindness and willingness to do such a favor for you. . . . He is a lover of Japan, but not a slave.' This speech pleased the commissioner exceedingly, and made every one in the room look at me. When he noticed me standing erect he asked Mr. Mori whether the corner-stander was Mr. Neesima.

When he ascertained that it was, he stepped forward from his seat, shook my hand, and made a most graceful yet most dignified bow to me, asking me to be a kind friend to him. He bowed himself sixty degrees from the perpendicular, so I made a like bow in return. I could not help laughing in my heart that a behind or corner stander was so honored by him. He gave me an order to be an interpreter to him when he goes around the country to examine the schools, and to tell him all about your school system. I told him if I am *ordered* to do this I would rather refuse it, because he should distinguish me from the others who received aid from the government; but if I am *requested* to do this for a certain compensation, I would gladly do any favor for him. The commissioner told Mr. Mori to treat and receive me exactly as I requested him."

Three days later he again writes at the close of a letter to Mr. and Mrs. Hardy: "My principal mission is to write an essay on 'The Universal Education of Japan.' I think it is a most important mission. It will be handed to the embassy, and probably may be of some service for opening the country to the light of truth and life. Pray for this untiring soldier of the blessed cross, for I feel my active battle-field has come within my sight. I am ready to march forward, not asking whether my powder is dried or not, but trusting simply and believing only that the Lord of Hosts will help me to do my duty."

Again, two weeks later: "I have been resting to-day, preparing myself for the coming Lord's Day; for if I overdo to-day I shall not be able to enjoy the service of the Sabbath."

Mr. Neesima now spent a year with the Japanese embassy, visiting all the capitals of Europe with them, and devoting all his energies to help them gain the information they desired. His "stableness" and firm Christian principle shone out during this visit to Europe. In most European countries the railroad trains run on the Sabbath the same as on any other day, and the embassy often traveled on that day; Mr. Neesima, however, never traveled with them on the Sabbath. He told the writer that he always stopped off Saturday night, alone, and followed on after them on Monday. He spoke of one of these experiences, when he stopped off one Saturday night, in France, among entire strangers, and not knowing French, he expected to have a lonely day; but he wandered about and succeeded in finding a place where a Christian service was being conducted, and, entering, found it was a communion service. He remained and partook of the communion with them, and although he could understand but very little, he spoke of it as among the most blessed experiences of his life.

By his faithfulness and his conscientious adherence to principle he gained the confidence of these men, a confidence which lasted till the day of his death; and when he came back to Japan and wished to start his school, these men were at the head of the government, and to his intimacy with them and their firm confidence in him the Doshisha University owes its existence.

Mr. Neesima's careful habit of looking into all the details of whatever came in his way to examine, and especially his great interest in education, which had led him to make a careful examination of the common-school system of the United States, had prepared him to be of invaluable service to the embassy and to his country. He wrote out a carefully prepared paper, which was taken as the basis of the report which the embassy made on education, and which was afterward modified and introduced into Japan, and is the foundation of the system of education in the empire to-day.

As the time drew near for the departure of the embassy from Europe, to return home by way of India, Mr. Neesima was pressed to accompany them to Japan, and it seemed that it would be almost impossible for him to refuse to do so; but an attack of rheumatism coming on at this time, and the fear of becoming entangled in an official life, led him to remain behind, among strangers, until long after the embassy had sailed for Japan; so that, on his recovery, he returned to his studies in Andover.

He was very retired and studious in his manner, although his intense thirst for knowledge would lead him to break over his reserve and seek information from his fellow-students. He was greatly afflicted with rheumatism during his last year in the seminary, and suffered from its effects at times during the rest of his life.

Being graduated in the summer of 1874, the questions of his return to Japan, what relation he should sustain to the American Board, his ordination, and his support, all came up for solution. It was finally decided that it was best that he should receive ordination before leaving for Japan, and a council of churches in the State where he had spent ten years was called. He passed a very satisfactory examination, and was ordained as an evangelist—the first of his race to take upon himself this office. He was also appointed a corresponding member of the Japan mission of the American Board. Mr. Hardy also arranged to have sent to Mr. Neesima each year what he needed for his support, so that he was placed above anxiety on that point.

The following extracts from Mr. Neesima's letter to the secretaries of the Board, formally offering himself as a missionary, and from his replies to the questions propounded to candidates for appointment, will show the spirit of the man, and how his mind stood with reference to theology.

"I date my conversion some time after my arrival in this country; but I was seeking God and his light from the hour I read his Word. With my new experience was born a desire to preach the Gospel among my people. The motive in offering myself to this work is my sympathy with the need of my country, and love for perishing souls; and, above all, the love of Christ has constrained me to this work."

"In my view, the leading doctrines of the Scriptures are: the existence of one true God, inspiration of the Scriptures, the Trinity, the decrees of God, the freedom of the will, the total depravity of man, the atonement, regeneration, justification by faith, the resurrection of the dead, the final judgment. I have not the least doubts respecting any of the doctrines commonly held by the churches sustaining the missions under the care of the Board. My confidence in the reality of my conversion is in my growing trust in Christ and increasing sympathy with truth. My views of ministerial duty are to preach the Gospel to the salvation of men. My desire to enter the ministerial work is due to the need of it in Japan, and my hope that I may be of some service in supplying that need. I expect to meet with some difficulties and trials, yet I shall count it all joy, not only to believe in Christ, but also to suffer for his name. It is my purpose to give my life to this work."

He was now ready to return to his loved land and friends, but there was still one thing which weighed upon his heart. He had come to America and seen for himself the light of Christian civilization; he had drunk deeply at the fountains of knowledge, and he felt an inexpressible longing to see such a fountain of true knowledge opened in his own land; he had not started on his world-wide quest for truth for himself—he came for the good of his people: should he go back with a full heart but with an empty hand? The same Hand which had so wonderfully led him to America, and which had taken care of him there and given him such a preparation for his work, led him farther to make an appeal which other hearts were ready to second, and so begin an enterprise which should be indeed a blessing to his whole people.

I quote here from Mr. Neesima's own words, written in a letter, the last one in English which his hand ever penned, written only a few days before his death. He says: "Fifteen years ago I had a day-dream to found a Christian college. I used to express my intense desire to found it, especially to raise up Christian workers, to Dr. Clark, secretary of the American Board, and also to some other friends, but none of them gave me any encouraging words. However, I was not discouraged at all. I kept it within myself and prayed over it.

"In the fall of 1874 I was invited to attend the annual meeting of said Board, which was held in Rutland, Vt., to bid my last farewell to my friends. I was ordered to appear on the platform on the very last day of the meeting. In the evening of the previous day I called on Mr. and Mrs. Alpheus Hardy, my benefactors, and consulted with them about the advisability of my bringing out my long-cherished scheme—that is, to found a Christian college in Japan—in my farewell speech. Mr. Hardy was rather doubtful about my attaining any success; however, I rather insisted, because it was my last chance to bring out such a subject to such a grand Christian audience. Then he spoke to me, half smiling, and in a most tender, fatherly manner said, 'Joseph, the matter looks rather dubious, but you might try it.' Receiving that consent I went back to the place where I was entertained and tried to make a preparation for the speech. I found my heart throbbing, and was utterly unable to make a careful preparation. I was then like that poor Jacob, wrestling with God in my prayers.

"On the following day, when I appeared on the stage, I could hardly remember my prepared piece—a poor, untried speaker; but after a minute or two I recovered myself, and my trembling knees became firm and strong; a new thought flashed into my mind, and I spoke something quite different from my prepared speech. My whole speech must have lasted less than fifteen minutes; while I was speaking I was moved with the most intense feeling over my fellow-countrymen, and I shed much tears, instead of speaking in their behalf. But before I closed my poor speech about five thousand dollars were subscribed on the spot to found a Christian college in Japan. That generous subscription of our American friends became the nucleus of the present Doshisha, which is now recognized as the best and largest Christian college in Japan."

The writer has heard from many persons who were present at that meeting that it was a scene never to be forgotten; the intense earnestness of this young Japanese, as he spoke of the great blessings of a Christian education, and pictured to them, with broken voice and overflowing eyes, the darkness and need of his own people; the evident nervousness of the secretaries at the manly appeal which was made, for the speaker said: "I cannot go back to Japan without the money to found a Christian college, and I am going to stand here till I get it." Then Governor Page of Vermont arose and said: "Put me down for one thousand dollars." Dr. Parker of Washington followed with five hundred dollars, Mr. Hardy with five hundred, William E. Dodge with five hundred, and others with lesser sums, until nearly five thousand dollars were raised.

# III

## LAYING FOUNDATIONS

"*Behold, I lay in Sion for a Foundation a Stone, a tried Stone, a precious Corner-stone of sure Foundation: he that believeth shall not make haste.*"—ISA. XXVIII. 16.

"*And not only so, but let us also rejoice in our tribulations: knowing that tribulation worketh patience; and patience, probation; and probation, hope: and hope putteth not to shame; because the love of God hath been shed abroad in our hearts through the Holy Ghost which was given unto us.*"—ROM. V. 3–5.

"*The good man does better than he knows.*"

"*Fasten your soul so high that constantly
The smile of your heroic cheer may float
Above the floods of earthly agonies.*"
E. B. BROWNING.

"*God's glory is a wondrous thing,
  Most strange in all its ways,
And, of all things on earth, least like
  What men agree to praise.*

"*Oh, blest is he to whom is given
  The instinct that can tell
That God is on the field when he
  Is most invisible!*

"*And blest is he who can divine
  Where real right doth lie,
And dares to take the side that seems
  Wrong to man's blindfold eye!*

"*Oh, learn to scorn the praise of men!
  Oh, learn to lose with God!
For Jesus won the world through shame,
  And beckons thee his road.*

"*And right is right, since God is God;
  And right the day must win;
To doubt would be disloyalty,
  To falter would be sin!*"
FABER.

# CHAPTER III

### LAYING FOUNDATIONS

MR. NEESIMA reached Japan in December, 1874. Great changes had taken place during his ten years of absence. The mikado was reinstated, his capital was changed from Kyoto—where his ancestors had ruled for a thousand years—to Tokyo; the daimios had relinquished their feudal rights, and the pensions of their retainers were capitalized; the Julian or Gregorian calendar had been adopted, and the Sabbath was made a holiday; the post-office, with a money-order system, a savings-bank system, and a postal delivery system, was established; newspapers were being printed and circulated; an army and a navy on a foreign plan were formed; a mint was established; the coast was being surrounded with lighthouses; the first railroads were opened; and a network of telegraphs was unifying the old feudal kingdom. Most of these changes had taken place one or two years before Mr. Neesima returned. The great question of constitutional liberty was beginning to be agitated, and the men whose confidence and love Mr. Neesima had gained in his intercourse with the embassy, three years before, were at the head of the government. Their prejudices had been removed and their minds broadened by their intercourse with Western nations, and they were ready to encourage the adoption of Western civilization in their own empire.

Mr. Neesima was offered, again and again, places of high position under these men, and urged to accept them, but he steadily declined. He allowed nothing to turn him from the great purpose of his life, to establish a Christian college in his native land.

Soon after Mr. Neesima established the school in Kyoto, a high official sent him a letter, from which I extract the following: "You have knowledge, you have wisdom, and, above all, you are still young. Why, then, are you retired in Kyoto, and passing your time with young boys and girls in leisure? It may be because you are so earnest in religion, but why do you not become a great public man, and extend your influence in the world?" Mr. Neesima replied as follows: "I am very thankful for your kind advice. But suppose I should take a government position, how much benefit could I give to Japan? Certainly very little. On the contrary, if I educate many young men and women here in this place of beautiful mountains and pure water, and produce hundreds and thousands of Neesimas who can work for this country, it will be of some benefit. This is the aim of my life."

Soon after landing in Yokohama he visited his aged parents, who had gone back to their native province, and were living in Annaka. There were at this time small churches in Tokyo, Yokohama, Osaka, and Kobe, but it was hardly safe to profess Christianity even in the open ports. Away from the open ports there was very little, if any, effort on the part of any Japanese to teach the forbidden doctrines. But no sooner did Mr. Neesima reach Annaka, seventy-five miles from Tokyo, than the people began to beg him to tell all about foreign countries, and he took that opportunity to openly tell them about Christianity; he did this so boldly for several days that the governor of that province became troubled. Mr. Neesima was plainly violating the old law, but yet he was no ordinary person · he had been attached to the Iwakura embassy, and was already a widely known man. To arrest or even caution him might have some unknown results; so the governor went hastily in person to Tokyo, and laid the matter before some of the men who were at the head of the government. They replied: "If it is Neesima, it is all right; let him alone;" so the governor returned satisfied, and a work was begun which resulted in the organization of the Annaka church a few years later under the labors of Mr. Yebina. The Annaka church, with the five other churches within a very few miles which have sprung from it, make it probably the most thoroughly evangelized community in Japan. Several of the members of the first provincial assembly and a majority of the standing committee were Christian men, and two thirds of the members of the first Imperial Diet elected from that province were Christians.

In a letter to Mr. Hardy, Mr. Neesima recites the experiences of this period as follows:

"It was my intention to remain in Yokohama for three days when I arrived there; but when once I stepped on the dry land—my dear native soil—I could not wait even for three days. Hence I hurried home without stopping in Tokyo. When I came here it was midnight; therefore I disliked to disturb my parents' sleep, and slept in an inn. In the morning I sent word to my father. Then I came home, and was welcomed by my aged parents, sisters, neighbors, and old acquaintances. My father had been ill for three days, and could not move himself, on account of rheumatism; but when he heard of my safe arrival he rose up and welcomed me with fatherly tenderness. When I hailed him he stooped down without a word. I noticed his tears dropping on the floor. My old acquaintances gathered at our home, and requested me to tell them all my experiences in the United States. The people came here from the surrounding towns, even seven or eight miles away. They have kept me busy all the time. They look as sheep without a shepherd. I found it almost impossible to send them back without giving them some spiritual food.

"Soon after my arrival home I presented your kind letter to my father, but for a long time I could not translate it for him, because when I tried to read it I could not help thinking of the scene of my last departure from you.

"Another day I gathered my parents and sisters, and succeeded in reading your letter to them. Before I got half through all of them began to weep, being much affected by your parental kindness to me. My father told me you were our saviors and our gods. Then I told him he must not make our American friends gods. If he feels grateful for their deeds he must worship that God, the only one God, the Creator of the universe, the Saviour of mankind, the God of his American friends. I mentioned, still further, that these friends became so good and kind, even to a wandering stranger, because they are true worshipers of God and the followers of Christ, who is, indeed, the Saviour of mankind. He came to this sinful world to save the poor and lost. These friends saved me from a miserable condition, and gave me necessary education, so that I might become a teacher of the glad tidings of salvation to our benighted people. Since that time my poor father has discontinued to worship the Japanese gods and his ancestors. By his consent I took down all the paper, wooden, earthen, and brass gods from shelves where they were kept, and burned them up. I send a few paper gods for you, which my mother threw into the fireplace. There

NEESIMA IN HAKODATE, 1864

are no gods or images in this house now. I trust they will be worshipers of the true God hereafter.

"Besides my home friends, my humble labors within three weeks have been wonderfully blessed. I have preached several times in the school-house, and also preached to small audiences in families. A week ago I preached to a large audience in a Buddhist temple. All the priests in this community came and listened to the preaching of the new religion. There were over two hundred present, consisting of priests, laymen, and a few women and children. At my preaching in the school-house the whole body of magistrates from the city of Takasaki came to hear me preach. One of my hearers went home and took down all his gods, and has ceased to worship them. Thirty men in this town, and a few men out of the town, took up a collection to buy some Christian books. One gave six dollars; the whole was $17.35. They requested me to buy the books. They are hungry and thirsty for the Christian truth. I find here everything ready for the Gospel."

On Mr. Neesima's visit to Annaka dates the entrance of Christianity into the heart of Japan, and that was the beginning of the fearless preaching of the Gospel in the interior.

After a few weeks spent with his friends in Annaka, preaching the Gospel, Mr. Neesima came on to Kobe and Osaka to confer in regard to the establishment of the Christian college.

A short time before Mr. Neesima's return our mission received a letter from Secretary Clark telling us that five thousand dollars were waiting to found a collegiate and theological training-school to train Christian workers for Japan. We had not yet begun to think of such a school, or at least we felt that it was far in the future. Our first two churches had been organized that year, one in Kobe with eleven members, and one in Osaka with seven members; a few young men were found ready to listen to the truth, also, in Sanda, twenty miles from Kobe; but the villages about Kobe and between Kobe and Osaka were so much opposed to Christianity that it was impossible to even teach a few men in an hotel, or tea-house.

Mr. Neesima tried for several months to secure permission from the governor of the Osaka-Fu to establish the college in that city. The governor told him he would approve the establishment of the school there, but that no missionary should teach in it; so Mr. Neesima reluctantly gave up hope in Osaka, and then our thoughts were turned to Kyoto. But Kyoto was an interior city, where foreigners had never been allowed to reside; it had been the center of Buddhism and Shintoism in Japan for a thousand years; and, moreover, it was away from the centers of work which our mission had opened.

The mission, however, gave a reluctant consent to the location of the school in Kyoto, if permission could be secured; and in the summer of 1875 Mr. Neesima went to Kyoto to see what could be done. The Lord had prepared the way before him; the city had been opened for one hundred days during the three previous years, while the exhibition was held there. Rev. O. H. Gulick had spent three months in the city during the summer of 1872, and had made the acquaintance of Mr. Yamamoto Kakuma, a blind man who was then a private counselor to the Kyoto-Fu. Others of our mission had met him during the next two summers, and he had become greatly interested in Christianity. When Mr. Neesima presented his plan for the establishment of a Christian college in Kyoto to Mr. Yamamoto, he was ready to give it his warm approval from the first, and he used his strong influence with the governor of the Kyoto-Fu in the same direction, so that the governor also gave his approval to the scheme.

The writer made a hasty visit to Kyoto in June of 1875, and, with Mr. Neesima, looked at a lot of land containing five and a half acres, 6500 tsubo, situated in the northern part of the city, just above the old palace grounds, and with a large temple grove of one hundred acres on the north side of it. This land was the former site of the palace of the Satsuma daimio, the last resident being Shimadzu Saburo. It was now in the possession of the blind Yamamoto, and he gladly sold it to us for the school for the sum of five hundred and fifty dollars.*

Thus the site for the school was secured. What should be its name? Many were thought of, but finally the name "Doshisha" was decided upon; this means one endeavor, or one purpose company. Mr. Neesima was in Kyoto all the summer of that year except during a hurried visit to Tokyo. Although the approval of the local government had been secured for the location of the school in Kyoto, the approval of the central government was necessary. A building must also be secured for the school, and permission for a missionary to reside in Kyoto and teach in the school. Mr. Neesima was busy with all these plans, and his heart was stirred also to find some way by which the Gospel could be freely taught in the school and in the city, and all over the empire.

He writes August 2d: "I had a most interesting interview with Mr. ——, a young man who is connected with the educational department at Tokyo. He told me that he would do his best to allow missionaries to be hired in

---

\* It is an interesting fact that Mr. Yamamoto was confined a prisoner in a low room on this very ground for two years during the war of the restoration, and was there attacked with that rheumatism which made him a cripple till the day of his death.

our Kyoto school; but for teaching Christianity in it, he has no power to say much, because as Christian religion it comes under Dai-kyo-in, or department of religion. I think it would not do for us to present this matter to Dai-kyo-in, because they will never do us any favor. So I think a best way will be to try to get religious freedom in the empire. I will write to our influential men in the cabinet and induce them to work for it. Mr. —— promised me to work for it privately among the radical statesmen. He rather asked me to come to Tokyo to see them myself. In the first place I must get a letter from my native province which will assure the Kyoto government that I belong to that ken, and will henceforth become a citizen of Kyoto. Then I can make my religious faith known to the Kyoto government; it will be the very first thing ever done in Kyoto. I think the Kyoto government will present the matter to the central government. If case requires, I will present myself to the central government; then, as I said above, in the mean time I will work privately for religious freedom among the radical statesmen. I think this is the only way to get Kyoto open for our Christian institution."

August 24th he writes: "I have already presented the petition for our school, and especially for hiring a missionary; and in order to gain the governor's favor I made a friendly call on him last night. He strongly advised me to go to Tokyo as soon as possible, or not any later than our petition reaches the central government. I am deliberately following the advice of the governor, who so recently came back from Tokyo and knows exactly the present state of things in the central government."

Mr. Neesima hurried off by jinrikisha overland to Tokyo, and reached there as soon as the petition did. He saw Mr. Tanaka, who was at the head of the department of education. Mr. Tanaka was Mr. Neesima's special friend, having become such while they were in Europe together. He told him, however, at first, that it would be impossible to grant permission for a Christian school to be opened in the city of Kyoto; it was regarded as the sacred city of the empire, and he feared great opposition and prejudice on the part of the people. Mr. Neesima saw him repeatedly during three days, and Mr. Tanaka finally told him that if he would be very careful not to do anything to arouse the opposition of the people he would grant the permission. Thus the permission was finally granted to open the school in Kyoto. Mr. Neesima also formed a company, consisting of himself and Mr. Yamamoto, to open the school, hire teachers, etc.; this company of two was the Doshisha for several years.

The writer having been engaged as the first foreign teacher in the school, Mr. Neesima wrote, October 11th, in regard to a house for my family and one for the school. In this letter he says: "I hope his reply will come within to-day. I think it is pretty early for me to say to-day—it is now 3.30 A.M. I awoke at a quarter before two o'clock, and could not sleep again, so I got up some time after two o'clock and wrote a pretty long letter to Mr. —— to get permission to rent his house. Can you do anything for this sleepless old fellow? I am exceedingly tired, but can't sleep." Again, October 16th, five days later, he writes: "I have been sleepless these past five nights, but I slept first-rate last night. I hope I shall do so again to-night. My hope for Kyoto was quite brightened up." The reason for his brighter hopes was that the permission for my residence in Kyoto, which had been pending so long, and for which he had been writing and telegraphing to Tokyo, had come, and the way was open for him to commence the school. He had had a long and anxious summer.

I entered Kyoto with my family October 19th, and settled down in a part of the old Yanagiwara yashiki on the east side of the imperial palace, and Mr. Neesima had a little house on Shin Karasumaru, above Maruta Machi. Mr. Neesima had a small company to whom he preached and taught the Bible in his own house each Sabbath all summer; I began a similar service in my house the first Sabbath we were in the city, and only six were present; but both audiences increased so that in a few weeks they numbered from thirty to sixty.

We had hardly entered the city, however, before the Buddhist priests held many meetings and finally sent a strong petition to the central government asking to have us expelled. I find written in my diary of November 19th: "The opposition of the priests is having its effect upon the officials of the city: they are less friendly. The acorn is in the bottle, however, and it will, in time, with God's blessing, split the bottle."

Mr. Neesima made applications about this time for Dr. Taylor and Dr. Learned to teach in the school, and he was very greatly tried for five months before they were granted. I will quote from my diary of Monday, November 22d, to show how he was tried: "Mr. Neesima has called several times during the last week or two to see the governor, but always found him not at home. Friday evening last he called again, and was told that he was too busy to see him; he went early Saturday morning, and was told that it was too early; he went a little later, and was told that the governor was about starting for the office; he inquired through the servant if he could see him in the evening, and was told that he could not promise; he went home, and yesterday he received notice to appear at the office this morning and explain what he meant by *Seisho*, Bible, in the list of studies as put forth in the program of the school." The only result of the sending of the strong petition of the priests to Tokyo, so far as we know, was that Mr. Tanaka, the head of the department of education, sent a request to the governor of Kyoto, asking that, for the present, we would not teach the Bible in the school. Mr. Neesima gave him a written promise to that effect on the 22d of November. The governor told him that we could teach Christianity in the school under the name of moral science, and teach everything there except Bible exegesis, and that we could teach that and preach in our homes. This request was made by Mr. Tanaka for fear of trouble in the city, as there was great excitement about our coming to open a Christian school. The owner of the building we had rented for the school had given Mr. Neesima notice that he wanted his house for himself, and that we could not have it; but after this Bible-teaching was arranged with the governor the owner concluded to let us have it.

From my diary, November 29, 1875: "We began our school this morning in Mr. Neesima's house at eight o'clock, with a prayer-meeting, in which all the scholars took part; then, going to the school-house, two others were received, making seven boarding scholars and one day-scholar." I never shall forget Mr. Neesima's tender, tearful, earnest prayer in his house that morning as we began the school; all prayed from the heart. December 4th we had twelve scholars. We worked on through the winter, the school growing gradually, until we had about forty scholars, the attendance at the Sabbath services increasing, until sixty or seventy were present. The passes for Drs. Taylor and Learned, which gave Mr. Neesima trouble all winter, were finally sent on to Tokyo, and granted in March, 1876.

# IV

## MARRIAGE, TRIALS, AND WORK

"*In love of the brethren be tenderly affectioned one to another; in honor preferring one another; in diligence not slothful; fervent in spirit; serving the Lord; rejoicing in hope; patient in tribulation; continuing steadfastly in prayer.*"—ROM. XII. 10–12.

> "*For marriage is a matter of more worth*
> *Than to be dealt in by attorneyship;*
> *For what is wedlock forced but a hell,*
> *An age of discord and continual strife;*
> *Whereas the contrary bringeth forth happiness,*
> *And is a pattern of celestial bliss.*"
> SHAKESPEARE.

> "*Sorrow and silence are strong,*
> *And patient endurance is godlike.*"
> LONGFELLOW.

> "*Leave God to order all thy ways,*
> *And hope in him, whate'er betide;*
> *Thou'lt find him in the evil days*
> *An all-sufficient strength and guide;*
> *Who trusts in God's unchanging love*
> *Builds on a rock that naught can move.*"
> GEORG NEUMARK.

> "*Life is real, life is earnest,*
> *And the grave is not its goal;*
> *'Dust thou art, to dust returnest,'*
> *Was not spoken of the soul.*
> . . . .
> "*Let us then be up and doing,*
> *With a heart for any fate:*
> *Still achieving, still pursuing,*
> *Learn to labor and to wait.*"
> LONGFELLOW.

> "*Blind unbelief is sure to err,*
> *And scan his work in vain;*
> *God is his own interpreter,*
> *And he will make it plain.*"
> COWPER.

# CHAPTER IV

## MARRIAGE, TRIALS, AND WORK

SOON after Mr. Neesima came to Kyoto he became acquainted with Yamamoto Yaye, a sister of the blind counselor of the Kyoto-Fu; and, meeting her repeatedly at her brother's house, acquaintance ripened into affection, and in the autumn of that year they were engaged.

On Sabbath, January 2, 1876, the Lord's Supper and also the ordinance of baptism were celebrated for the first time in the city, at the regular service at my house. Yamamoto O Yaye received baptism at that time, and the next day, January 3d, in the presence of all the members of our school, of the ex-daimio of Tango and his daughter, of several friends whom we had made in the city, and of Mr. Yamamoto's family, Mr. Neesima and O Yaye were united in marriage. This proved a very happy union, and Mr. Neesima had a faithful, loving wife during all the years until God called him up higher.

In the letters he wrote us from America, while there in 1885, it was very touching to see how much he felt the separation from Mrs. Neesima, and how he also remembered to ask us to help her bear her loneliness.

Mr. Sears, a wealthy Boston gentleman, whose acquaintance Mr. Neesima made while in the United States, sent out a sum of money for Mr. Neesima to use to build him a comfortable home, and also another sum to build a chapel.

He secured a large lot on Teramachi, above Maruta Machi, and there built a home for himself. It was several years before we could secure any places in the city for preaching, and a service was held at Mr. Neesima's house, and the school met at my house each Sabbath afternoon for more than two years. At this latter preaching service more than two hundred people often gathered to hear the Gospel, and, as the house became too small, the money given by Mr. Sears was used to build a chapel near by. Mr. Neesima used often to preach in those days, and his sermons were intensely earnest and impressive.

To show the difficulty we encountered in trying to teach Christianity at this time one example may be given. A physician in Fushimi, a southern suburb of Kyoto, asked us to come down to his house and teach the Gospel; the writer went down one Sabbath and gave him and a few of his friends who had assembled in his house a talk about the true God; the next Sabbath Mr. Neesima went down and talked to the five or six people who assembled; for this the physician was summoned to appear at the Kyoto-Fu, and told that he must not allow such meetings at his house. All who had listened or who had received any tracts were also summoned to appear at the office, and very closely questioned and frightened. The physician was thus summoned on three separate occasions.

The following is a part of the conversation which occurred between the Fu officials and this physician on the last day, when he was discharged: "This Davis came up here to teach an English school, did he not?" "Yes." "Then he is like a man who has a license to sell deer meat, but who sells dog meat?" "Well, is it dog meat? I used to think so, but on tasting of it I find it is a great deal better than deer meat; and I would like to ask you one question: this way is allowed to be taught publicly in

NEESIMA'S WIFE AND MOTHER

Kobe, in Osaka, and in twenty or thirty places in Tokyo; how is it that here, in the Kyoto-Fu, a man is not allowed to hear it in his own house? Are we not all under the same government? I do not understand it." "Well," says the official, "I do not say that way is either good or bad, and I do not say that you and your friends cannot hear it in your house; but you let in the common people, the lower classes, who cannot understand it; we cannot allow this. We have good and sufficient religions here in Japan—we do not want any more; we have Confucianism for the scholars like you, and Buddhism for the masses." The doctor replied: "I would like to ask you one thing: If Confucianism is an all-sufficient religion, why is it, since its founder lived hundreds of years before Christ, and taught during a long life, that this way has not spread beyond China and Japan? So if Buddhism is an all-sufficient religion, started by Buddha hundreds of years before Christ, and taught by him through a long life, how is it that it has not spread beyond India, China, and Japan? And if Christianity is a bad way, how is it, since its founder only taught three years, and was put to death when he was thirty-three years old, that it has spread all over Europe and America, and is spreading all over Africa and Asia and all the islands of the sea?" "Well, we do not say that it is either good or bad, but you must not allow people to meet at your house, and you are discharged," replied the official. The physician came from the Fu right to my house and told me this, and I copied it into my diary. He borrowed a quantity of books and tracts, took them home, and lent them to his neighbors; but his practice gradually fell off, and he came near to starvation, so prejudiced did the people become against him; and he finally lost his interest in Christianity.

This opposition on the part of officials, and the fact

that the Bible was not allowed to be taught in the school, caused much dissatisfaction in the mission, so that after the permission for Drs. Taylor and Learned had been granted, and before they moved into the city, about the middle of March, a special meeting of the mission was called in Osaka, and half a day was spent over the question of abandoning Kyoto, and locating the school where the missionaries could be free to live and to teach the Bible. Although one of the mission afterward said it was "the most reluctant vote the mission ever gave," the vote was given to remain, none dissenting. A few months later, the last of June, a vote was given by the mission to approve of the erection of two buildings on the ground bought for the school. It was a very reluctant vote, but the fact that most thought it very doubtful if the erection of the buildings would be allowed by the government helped the doubtful ones, and the vote was given, none dissenting; one brother said, however, "Brethren, you may just as well try to fly to Mars as to try to put up those buildings; it will not be allowed." In just three months and twenty days from that time this brother sang in the new buildings, "We'll hold the fort," etc., and took part in the exercises of dedication.

As the buildings stood completed, and the day appointed to open the school in them drew near, the temporary restriction in regard to the Bible still held. Many of the members of the mission were greatly exercised about opening the training-school of the mission in the new buildings; some were in favor of demanding the removal of the restriction, and, in case it was refused, then of abandoning everything—buildings, work, and all—and of leaving the city. One brother wrote: "We have no training-school; the school that will begin next week will not be the training-school," etc. Another brother wrote that he did not believe that we would be allowed to teach the Bible and pray in the school for three or five years, perhaps not for fifteen or twenty years yet.

Within one of a majority of the members of the mission signed a call for a special meeting to reconsider the whole question of the location of the school in Kyoto, and decide whether we should open the school in the new buildings. One member of the mission had just started overland to Tokyo, and was at this very time weather-bound by a three days' storm of wind and rain, and wondering why he was permitted to start. Had he been within reach the meeting would have been called, and no one can predict what would have been the result. But the meeting was not called, and after consultation with Mr. Yamamoto it was decided, since the excitement in the city had completely subsided, to dedicate the new buildings with religious exercises, to have morning prayers in the chapel, to open all the recitations of the theological department with prayer, and to teach all the studies and give all the lectures of the theological department, except Bible exegesis, in the new building, and to secure a third building in Mr. Neesima's name for the exegesis. The new buildings were dedicated on the morning of September 18, 1876; they consisted of what are now known as dormitories No. 1 and No. 2. The exercises consisted of a prayer of invocation, reading the Scriptures, sketch of the founding of the school, prayer of dedication, addresses in Japanese and English, and the singing of two hymns in Japanese and three in English.

At this time Mr. Neesima wrote as follows to Mr. and Mrs. Hardy: "I must express my heartfelt thanks to you for your having led and educated me in such a way that I might found a Christian institution on my dearly beloved soil. As you know we started our school in a hired house, but, having found this very inconvenient, we began the process of building two months ago. The buildings are three in number, two of which contain recitation-rooms and twenty-four rooms for students, while the other is a small structure and is used for a dining-room and kitchen. They are simple but solid, and look very pretty in the open space about them. We were permitted to dedicate them to the Lord the day before yesterday. . . . All but two of our Kyoto mission were present, and about seventy students, besides others from outside. Mr. Yamamoto's remarks were wonderfully appropriate. He is regarded as one of our best thinkers, although bodily feeble and helpless. The existence of the Kyoto mission is largely due to him. He was convinced that an immoral country like Japan could not be purified by any other means than Christianity, and by his influence and labor the proud and dignified governor listened to us, and at last smiled upon our efforts. In the dark and trying hours of last winter he stood up for us and did his best to persuade the governor. The latter made no interference with our dedication exercises. You will be glad to know that of our forty-seven boarding students more than half are Christians. They have come to us with the purpose of studying the Bible and fitting themselves for the ministry. We are very fortunate to get such pupils at the outset. I pray that this school may be the nucleus of a future college and university for Japan. Our mission work has also bright prospects, the work being chiefly carried on by our students. A third church will soon be formed. My aged parents now worship God instead of idols, and my invalid sister, who grasps spiritual things faster than these aged ones, takes part in the prayer-meetings for women held at my house. My wife attends the biblical exercises in the school. We are perfectly happy together, and I am try-

FIRST THEOLOGICAL HALL, DOSHISHA UNIVERSITY

ing to make my home like the Christian home I found in America."

Earlier than this Mr. Neesima had written to Mr. and Mrs. Hardy: "We are hated by the magistrates and priests, but we have planted the standard of truth here, and *will never more retreat*. To no one else but you will I say that this Christian school could have no existence here if God had not brought this poor runaway boy to your kind hands. The only way to get along in this country is to work courageously, even under many difficulties."

The first theological hall, shown in the engraving, was used for Bible-teaching for several years, until this could be taught in the regular school-buildings. This old "No. 30," as it was called, was a great contrast to the present beautiful theological hall, the gift of Mrs. Clarke of Brooklyn, in memory of her son. (See p. 100.)

The following extracts from letters written by members of the mission in 1875-76 will show how much the mission valued the work and influence of Mr. Neesima at this time: "Your contribution of Mr. Neesima to our mission and the cause of Christ in Japan is one whose value we feel no multiple of the sum you have invested in his education can represent. We are charmed by his thoroughly Christian spirit. . . . I cannot say a tithe of what is in my heart. . . . There seems no doubt but that his whole life, being, and purpose are consecrated to the Master for the redemption of his people. . . . He is profoundly grateful to you and to the American Board for what you and it have done for him and his land; and he accepts the will of the board and of our mission as God's will, no matter how it differs from his own. . . . If he is guided aright by God's Spirit, and kept firm to his purpose and work, if his health is spared, I feel that he is destined to accom-

plish as much, perhaps, as all our mission put together.
. . . We need him for a larger place than a pastorate.
We need him as a teacher in the training-school. He is
better fitted for some department of teaching than any
foreigner ever can be. We also need him as an evangelist—not to use his influence always in the same place, but
to go about awakening interest. . . . For a long time
after his return we feared he would break entirely down.
He was able to sleep but very little. He told me several
times during those first few months that when he thought
about these millions of his people passing into eternity
without a knowledge of Christ, it seemed as if he would
go crazy. Since the opening of the year he has gradually
improved, and is sleeping better. This is partly due to
the successful starting of the school, and his steady work
there; but largely, also, to his marriage and settlement in
a happy home of his own."

The constant opposition on the part of the Kyoto-Fu to
the school, the fact that the Bible could not be taught in
the school-buildings, and that so large a number of the mission were not satisfied to have the school opened and carried on in the new buildings, etc., led to continued criticism
of the school, and also to criticism of Mr. Neesima as the
virtual Japanese head of the school. He felt these most
keenly. He loved the members of the Japan mission, and
he was ever loyal to it; and anything which seemed to imply the contrary pained him beyond measure. So great did
the trial become that in September, 1876, the members of
the station sent a letter to the members of the mission to try
to remove some of these misunderstandings. I will quote
a few words from that letter, as they bring out one of Mr.
Neesima's remarkable characteristics: "Still farther, Mr.
Neesima and Mr. Yamamoto, as the nominal proprietors
of the school, so far from interfering with our manage-

ment of the school, have from the first left everything in our own hands; the exercises of the dedication, the manner of conducting morning prayers, what to teach, when to teach, how to teach, the employment of Japanese teachers, the ringing of the bell, the management of the food —all these things, instead of being suggested by them, have been suggested by us, and none of them even referred to Mr. Yamamoto at all, and not half of them to Mr. Neesima; and yet, so far as we know, Mr. Neesima has never hinted or thought a word of complaint, or asked that anything be changed. He even comes to us to consult about all the little details of his own classes. He has not expended a cent of the money which has been sent to him to use as he pleased for the school without first consulting us, and he has then invariably followed out our suggestions. We have been as free to run the school to suit ourselves, from our first connection with it, as if there had been no Japanese proprietors, or as if it had been located in Chicago." This can almost as truly be said after fourteen years as after one year.

We must now notice at some length another wonderful work—hardly less wonderful than the calling and preparation of Mr. Neesima. In the month of February, 1876, in the darkest days of that first winter, when the opposition was so great that it often seemed as if we must fail of our object of establishing a school in Kyoto, the writer received a large letter by the Japanese post. The handwriting was strange; the name, too, was strange. It was written from the old castle town of Kumamoto, in the middle of the island of Kiushu, by Captain L. L. Janes. In it he asked if we could receive into our school a number of earnest Christian young men, graduates of his school, to fit them for work as preachers of the Gospel. We did not know that such a man was in existence; we did not know that such a school was in existence. How did all this happen?

The following is a translation (made by a Japanese) of an account of the work of Captain Janes, prepared by Paul Kanamori, one of his pupils, who was a leading member of the Kumamoto Band:

"In 1871, Captain L. L. Janes came to Kumamoto upon the invitation of the daimio of Higo, and established a school where foreign knowledge was to be taught. The daimio was decided in his desire for a military officer, because he feared that if he employed an ordinary scholar the youths of the province would fall into literary weakness, and so the bold spirit of the province would be lost. So he employed this learned and valorous officer in order to introduce the sciences of the West, and at the same time stimulate the military spirit of the young men.

"Captain Janes having been employed with this end in view, his circumstances were very different from those of the missionaries. At that time Japan was still unenlightened, particularly in the vicinity of Kumamoto. The number of men who were yet opposed to Christianity was very great, so that even the lives of Captain and Mrs. Janes were by no means free from danger. The pupils were largely sons of the rough and turbulent men of the place, and it may be readily seen that to teach Christianity to them was a very delicate and difficult task. No pupil could understand English, and Captain Janes did not understand the Japanese language, so that the difficulty of communication was extreme.

"For the first two or three years Captain Janes said little or nothing about Christianity, but gave his whole strength to teaching English and the sciences; but he was so kind and fatherly in his treatment of his pupils that they came to forget that he was a foreigner, and they gladly listened to whatever he said to them.

"As he was a fervent Christian his desire to preach to the pupils must have been intense; but under the circumstances he wisely contented himself with first seeking to win his pupils' hearts as the best possible preparation for the future sowing of the Gospel seed. After he had been there about three years he one day said to us, 'I shall teach the Bible on Sunday; any one who wishes may come to my house.' We still hated Christianity as though it were a snake, and did not like even to see a Bible; but we so respected him that we concluded to go to the meeting. One of us went to the teacher of Chinese and asked his consent. He replied that we might go to learn about Christianity, not to believe it, but to study its strong and weak points in order to oppose it. And so, of the few who went, some went simply out of curiosity, others for amusement, others that they might oppose—none with a desire to accept it. The portions of the New Testament that we read had no flavor for us, and the time seemed spent in vain. But our teacher was kind and assiduous in his teaching, and fervent in his prayers for us. During his prayer, which seemed tedious to us, we sometimes opened our eyes and looked upon his face with its closed and tearful eyes, and then we laughed, saying that 'Americans weep.' At this time he simply taught the Bible, and never exhorted us to become Christians; and when two of us thought to impose upon him by pretending that we wished to become preachers, he met them sternly, saying, 'You are not yet worthy to become preachers; go on with your Bible study.' A year later, in 1875, a few were really touched by the Gospel, and this was followed by a division of the students into two parties, the one favorable to

Christianity, the other seeking to oppose it by reviving the study of 'The Great Learning' and 'The Doctrine of the Mean,' as taught by the Chinese sages. In August of the same year, Captain Janes added preaching to his biblical instruction. His sermons were long—sometimes three hours long—but as we had become interested in Christianity they were never tiresome to us. All who attended these meetings were studying the Confucian morality at the house of the Chinese teacher every Sunday afternoon, and so, for a while, we were studying Christianity with Captain Janes in the mornings and Confucianism with the Chinese teacher in the afternoons. For about six months we were thus divided in our admiration for Christianity and Confucianism, but by the end of the year all except one or two were united in their belief in Christianity.

"By Captain Janes's advice some of us spent the New Year's vacation in the study of the Gospel of John, and in prayer to God for his blessing upon ourselves and our classmates. [When the new term opened these Christian students had a faith which burned like fire, so that they could not but preach to their fellow-students and try to lead them to the gate of salvation. The whole school was like a boiling caldron; the studies were neglected, and groups of five, six, or seven men began to study the Bible in the recitation-rooms, the dining-room, or in their private rooms. These students had but little knowledge of the Bible or of theology, but they were impelled to preach, even though some of them were not more than twelve years old. The recitations were suspended, and Captain Janes gave himself to the work of preaching the Gospel to the students. We had not even heard of the word 'revival,' and knew nothing of the special workings of the Holy Spirit. We wondered why our spirits burned like a fire, and why we preached the Gospel like madmen. One said, 'May not this be the work of the Holy Spirit mentioned in the Bible?' And others answered, 'Yes, it may be.' Our preaching was not confined to the school, but found its way to the servants of the teachers, our kindred in our homes, old men and women in the streets, and so on.

"Now I must speak of one who was secretly praying in her closet, who received an open reward from her Heavenly Father. This was Mrs. Janes. She had no acquaintance with the students, but for many months her mind had been filled with intense desire for the salvation of the students, and she prayed day and night for the Holy Spirit to come upon them. This was the hidden cause of the revival. This revival continued for about a month, and those who confessed faith in Christ numbered over forty, and more than forty others were studying the Bible. On the last Sunday in January (January 30, 1876), a beautiful springlike day, the Christian students went out to a hill, Hana-oka-yama, southwest of Kumamoto—a hill since made famous as the spot where Saigo Takamori placed his cannon to bombard Kumamoto. They went singing hymns as they climbed the hill, and, taking their seats in a circle on its summit, they made a solemn covenant together, that as they had been thus blessed by God in advance of all their countrymen, they would labor to enlighten the darkness of the empire by preaching the Gospel, even at the sacrifice of their lives. 'They prayed kneeling, and wrote an oath-paper, on which they signed and sealed their names.'

"The fact that this covenant had been made became known, and all those connected with the school cried out in dismay, 'Alas! the students have become Christian priests. Captain Janes has made Christians of them. If this be not stopped our hopes for the school will be gone.'

"At this time the life of Captain Janes was in great danger, and the Christian students were persecuted in a thousand ways, for Christianity was looked upon as a kind of witchcraft.  One mother said to her son, 'If you don't abandon Christianity I must kill myself in order to wipe out the stain which you have cast upon your ancestors.' A father said, 'If you don't give up your faith I will kill you immediately.'  One student was confined in his room for one hundred days, and was finally driven from home. There was not one who was not more or less persecuted. On this account the number fell off to less than thirty. But the true believers, although the oldest was under twenty years of age, were immovable in their faith, and ready even to sacrifice their lives.  They were constantly encouraged and comforted by Captain Janes, and enabled to stand against the persecutions, which continued for about six months; so that the believers not only gained the victory, but were made all the stronger by their persecutions.  By the following autumn, Captain Janes left Kumamoto, and the Christians went to the Doshisha school in Kyoto, to prepare themselves more fully for the preaching of the Gospel."

The following is a translation of the covenant referred to, which was drawn up and signed by the Kumamoto Band at this time:

"When we first studied the Western religion we were greatly impressed, and as we afterward studied it more we were still more impressed, and were impelled to accept it with great joy; and now we wish to spread this religion in this empire, and thus enlighten the ignorance of the people.  The fact, however, that the people do not understand the wonderful doctrine of the Western religion, and so obstinately hold to their old opinions, is a great sor-

RECITATION HALL, DOSHISHA UNIVERSITY

row. At this time, if any one has patriotism, he ought to rise up with enthusiasm and account his life as dust, and bear witness to the catholicity and greatness of the Western religion. This is what we ought to do with all our might. Therefore, holding the same principles, we meet together on Hana-oka-yama and affirm our desire to work together for this religion with one accord.

"1. Those who have entered this religion must unite together with brotherly love, and mutually watch over and approve each other, separating from evil and cleaving to good; and thus practically show forth our faith by our works.

"2. If, after once entering this way, one does not follow it, he lies against God and deceives his own heart; such an one will certainly receive punishment from God.

"3. At the present time, since many of the people of this empire deny the Western religion, if one of our number wanders from this way he will not only deserve the public reproach, but we shall finally fail of obtaining our great purpose; hence how careful should we be to fulfil this pledge!

"HANA-OKA-YAMA, January 30, 1876, Sabbath."

As showing the spirit of the man who was the instrument in God's hands to do this wonderful work, and also some phases of that work, I will quote from some of Captain Janes's letters received during those trying months. In his first letter, dated February 7, 1876, he says: "My work in the school has been accompanied, from the time when it was possible to speak of Christianity, by constant and direct religious instruction of my pupils; in fact, the whole work has been inspired from the first with the one aim, on my part, of making it, under God, subserve the founding and upbuilding here of the kingdom of Christ, and so the highest welfare of those committed to my instruction and the large community influenced by them and the school." Again he writes, March 4th: "Meantime, my boys and I have been passing through unusual events, to say the least; and the mutterings of a sharp, vindictive, and exciting persecution are still in the air around us." "I think the little colony is practically intact; no lives have been taken, though that was threatened seriously enough; and there are no cases of *hara-kiri* yet to report, though a mother in one family and a father in another took that method of driving their sons from the faith; their degradation was declared to be insupportable." "I grieve over my imprisoned Christian boys. The physical strength of one is failing, and the unthinking persecutors may kill him. I understand there was an auto da fe of his Bibles a few days since."

Again, May 25th: "They blame me here, by implication, for educating preachers; I say nothing, but I have come to see that they need preachers and teachers of the 'True Light' more than any other educated workmen. The sham civilization they would build of a film of Western materialism dignified by the name of science and civilization, leaving the soul and all its needs unprovided for, is a hollow bubble that will burst one of these days. It is easy enough to kick a hole through it now; and unless the successive accretions are made to crystallize around the central principles of truth, justice, and liberty, and a wisdom large enough to satisfy the soul—Christ, the soul's want; God, the soul's author; and immortality, the soul's destiny—why, I don't know but the old nursery style were better than the violent ruptures and fearful reaction that must occur till the higher plane of progress is reached."

Here are also a few words from a letter Captain Janes sent up by the first one of his graduates who started for

Kyoto, dated June 25, 1876: "He was one of the first to see the light, to be convinced of the saving power of Christianity, and to give his heart unalterably to Jesus, 'all to leave and follow him;' and as a consequence he has been subjected to the most cruel and outrageous treatment at the hands of his brother, and has endured an imprisonment of some one hundred and twenty days. He was made the slave of the servants of his family, who were instructed to treat him as devil-possessed, without human rights. He is now practically an outcast. He is as a shorn lamb; he is leaving all."

In September fifteen graduates of Captain Janes's school, and as many more under-graduates, entered our school. These graduates were most of them virtually cast off by their friends for their faith in Christ, and they came to us with the clothes they wore and an English Bible as their sole earthly possessions. They found the school poorly organized, and were at first much dissatisfied. Captain Janes, however, encouraged them to stay, and they remained, and spent three years in theological study, supporting themselves by teaching the younger classes in the school, and graduating from the theological department in June, 1879. Three of them were retained as teachers in the school, and the others went out as teachers and preachers, and have been among the best Christian workers in Japan for the last ten years; Mr. Kosaki in Tokyo, Mr. Yebina in Joshu, Mr. Miyagawa in Osaka, Mr. Kanamori in Okayama, and Mr. Ise in Shikoku, have done work which has changed the history of Japan already. Five of these men are now connected with the school as teachers. Their coming into the school at that early day gave a Christian tone to the school, and their influence was felt in molding the Doshisha morally, and in shaping its course of study. They have helped to make the school what it is, and they came to love Mr. Neesima and to be loved by him as brothers.

The school gradually increased in numbers, so that during the third school year we had over one hundred students. Such was the feeling of opposition in Kyoto, however, that we had very few students from the city during the first five years; nearly half of them came from the island of Kiushu, led by the example and influence of the Kumamoto Band.

The opposition on the part of the officials in Kyoto grew stronger and stronger. December 23, 1877, Mr. Neesima wrote: "I wish to inform you of a recent event which happened in Kyoto. My brother-in-law, the blind Yamamoto, lost his connection with the Kyoto-Fu yesterday; I believe he lost his connection with the Fu on account of his connection with us." In the winter of 1879 Dr. Learned's permission to reside in Kyoto and teach in the school had nearly expired; if his permission was not renewed it would leave only one foreign teacher in the school; the requests made by the Doshisha for others to teach in the school had been refused, and Mr. Neesima was very anxious, during those months, about the very existence of the school. It was only after repeated solicitation with the Fu authorities here, and a visit to Tokyo and a personal interview with Mr. Mori, then at the head of the foreign department, that Dr. Learned's permit was finally obtained.

The whole situation during these first years was a great strain upon Mr. Neesima. Some of his best Japanese friends told him he was ruining his influence by receiving the money for his support from his benefactor, Mr. Hardy, and advised him to refuse to receive it and try to support himself. He was at one time inclined to yield to the criticisms of his friends, and refuse to receive Mr.

Hardy's benefaction longer. On one occasion, when all these trials seemed to be crushing him, he said to the writer with strong crying and tears, "Oh, that I could be crucified once for Christ, and be done with it!" This opposition lasted about six years, and seriously affected his general health.

The following is an extract from one of his letters to Mr. Hardy: "I must be thankful for the wise management of the American Board in sustaining our Kyoto institutions. Let the present arrangement continue as long as it may be needful. According to your kind fatherly advice I will be careful, and try to do all things in a perfect harmony with our missionaries. I shall be careful not to find fault in others. We were terribly attacked by some brethren in other stations. I attempted to defend our position. It is all over now. I shall say nothing about them, of them, or against them. There is now perfect harmony between the different stations of our mission. The last two months were the hardest ones I have ever experienced since my return to Japan. I found myself in the lowest stratum, and received the whole pressure upon myself. A heavy trial with respect to the government, and grave troubles among our native brethren, and also in our school. Oh, heavy burdens! I bore them chiefly on myself by His help, but I think I came pretty near to burst up my brains."

One trouble with the government to which he refers above was that they were exceedingly averse to having a school in Kyoto which was supported with foreign money, unless that fund were given directly to the Doshisha company; and in November, 1879, on returning from Annaka, Mr. Neesima received the good news that the appropriation for the school for the next year had been placed in the hands of the Doshisha company. The joy and relief which this brought were inexpressible. He wrote to Mr. Hardy, December 27, 1879: "I found your last letter on my arrival home. When I read it I exclaimed, 'The good Lord has done it!' My rejoicing was mingled with running tears. I knelt down before the Lord with my wife, and gave him our heartfelt thanks. Next to the Lord I must express my gratitude to you for your deep interest in us. I must also thank the gentlemen of the Board. Through this action I shall be relieved from grave difficulty. Step by step the plots of our enemies are defeated. 'Delight thyself in the Lord; and he shall give thee the desire of thy heart. Commit thy way unto the Lord; trust also in him; and he shall bring it to pass.' Oh, what precious promises they are unto us! I am wondering why God has chosen a weak instrumentality such as I am, weak both in body and mind, for promoting his kingdom in this empire. I could simply say to him, 'Here I am; employ me in thy vineyard if thou findest a pleasure in thy humble servant.' In my later experience I find more than ever nothingness in me."

In 1876 a school for girls was opened in the house of one of the missionaries, in which Mrs. Neesima and Miss Starkweather taught, and about two years later it was removed to its present location in a building erected for that purpose. The care of all this school work as it grew larger and larger, and the great number of outside calls which came upon Mr. Neesima, were a perpetual strain. Then, again, Mr. Neesima's reputation as one of the few men who had been thoroughly educated abroad, and his connection with the Iwakura embassy, brought many callers to his house, and occupied a great deal of his time; he was also consulted in regard to church work and missionary work, and in difficulties which arose in the churches or between individuals.

His heart was always warmly interested in the rapid spread of the Gospel in Japan, and he made many missionary tours himself, and earnestly proclaimed the Gospel. He wrote from Tokyo, February 13, 1879, a letter from which the following is an extract: "I started for Annaka on last Friday morning at three o'clock A.M." This was in the *basha*, or wagon, which at that time ran between Tokyo and Annaka. "It was then snowing, and I found myself chilled through. I reached Annaka toward evening; although I found myself rather tired I was obliged to receive quite a number of visitors that evening; then on Saturday the visitors poured in from the early morning, and there was scarcely a time for me to rest till the evening. We held a prayer-meeting on that evening. There were two candidates for baptism; the meeting lasted more than two hours. Another church meeting was held on Sunday morning. In the afternoon I preached in the usual way and officiated at the Lord's Supper. In the evening we held a prayer-meeting; it was a very warm and lively meeting and lasted more than two hours. I was so excited by the meeting that I could not sleep at all. At 12.30 A.M. on Monday morning I left Annaka on a coach, and reached Tokyo at 1.30 P.M. I am glad to say that the Annaka church is growing, and before the summer there may be half a dozen candidates for baptism. I have taken cold ever since I went to Annaka." He took this ride of nearly a hundred miles, and thus hurried back, because he had had a weighty case of arbitration put into his hands in Tokyo, which he must attend to that Monday afternoon.

Mr. Neesima, during those years, usually attended the business meetings of the mission, and also the prayer-meeting in English of the station, it being held once a week in turn at our houses, his house having its turn with the rest. We shall never forget his simple, earnest prayers in English at those meetings. He taught classes in the school in the early years, and he always gained the deep love of his pupils and of all who came in close contact with him; his silent influence in the school was very strong and pervasive. He also took an active part in the formation of the Japanese Home Missionary Society, connected with the Congregational churches, was its first president, and had a large part in superintending its work for many years.

# V

BROADENING PLANS—TOUR ABROAD

"*Commit thy way unto the Lord; trust also in him; and he shall bring it to pass.*"—Ps. XXXVII. 5.

> "*Rest is not quitting the busy career;
> Rest is the fitting of self to one's sphere.*"

> "*Build thee more stately mansions, O my soul,
> As the swift seasons roll!
> Leave thy low-vaulted past!
> Let each new temple, nobler than the last,
> Shut thee from heaven with a dome more vast,
> Till thou at length art free,
> Leaving thine outgrown shell by life's unresting sea.*"
> O. W. HOLMES.

> "*In the world's broad field of battle,
> In the bivouac of life,
> Be not like dumb, driven cattle—
> Be a hero in the strife.*
>
> . . . . . . .
>
> "*Trust no future, howe'er pleasant!
> Let the dead past bury its dead!
> Act—act in the living present,
> Heart within and God o'erhead!*"
> LONGFELLOW.

## CHAPTER V

BROADENING PLANS—TOUR ABROAD

IN the year 1883 Mr. Neesima began to think and plan actively to enlist interest among Japanese friends in the establishment of a university, or in the broadening out of the Doshisha into a Christian university. Up to this time the school had only been known in Japan as a Christian school, and the general idea among the leading men in the empire was that it was a school simply for training Christian preachers and evangelists; this was the very natural conclusion from the fact that most of the graduates up to that time had engaged in active Christian work. For this reason it was a very difficult matter to appeal for help for the school; but Mr. Neesima never swerved from his great purpose of a Christian school, nor from stating that publicly in his appeals. It was important to show the public that something besides the Bible and theology was taught in the school, and that its aim was a broader one than simply the training of evangelists; but it was always made very clear that the foundation of the school was Christian, and that Christianity was the foundation of the morality taught in it.

The writer was present at the first public meeting held for the purpose of awakening an interest in the university among the Japanese; it was held in a large hall in Kyoto, in the spring of 1884. About fifty of the officials and leading business men of the city were present, and Mr.

Neesima, Professor Ichihara, and the writer each addressed the meeting. Professor Ichihara's speech was one of the most ringing appeals for Christianity as the necessary foundation of all education to which I ever listened. The printed appeals which were made later speak for themselves.

The following is a free translation of the first general appeal for the university. It was prepared by Mr. Neesima and Mr. Yamamoto, and issued in May, 1884.

"The recent political changes in Japan have swept away feudalism, which has been the basis of society for many hundred years; and the influence of these changes has grown stronger and stronger until the society of Japan is very greatly changed. It appears like a new Japan. There are many who say that the government, the education, the commerce, and the industries which have existed in Japan must be improved. We heartily agree with their purpose as right and important to our civilization; but at the present time, when we look carefully at the condition of the country, there is one thing which gives us great sorrow. What is that? It is that there does not exist in Japan a university which is founded upon the most pure morality, and which teaches the new science. This is a necessary foundation of our civilization. In natural beauty and natural advantages Japan is not inferior to Europe and America. Why, then, is its civilization so different from theirs? It is also certain that there are in Japan but few noted men of earnest purpose. Hence we need universities in Japan.

"We can learn from the examples which Europe gives us. In the sixteenth century the great leader, Luther, said, 'If parents or brothers refuse to send children to school they are enemies of the state, and they ought to be punished.' The learned German, Fichte, said, 'The reason

LIBRARY HALL, DOSHISHA UNIVERSITY

that our nation stands first in civilization among the countries of Europe is in the power which comes from our universities.' The twelfth century was the dawning period of European civilization. At that time Greek philosophy was studied in the Paris University. In Italy the ancient Roman laws were studied in the University of Bologna. Between that time and the year 1600 the universities of Oxford and Cambridge were founded in England, Edinburgh and Glasgow in Scotland, Prague, Heidelberg, Leipsic, Tubingen, and Jena in Germany, and Dublin University was founded in Ireland. Besides these, universities have been founded in Holland, Spain, Portugal, and Austria.

"Abelard, Roger Bacon, Kepler, Galileo, Lord Bacon, Locke, Newton, Milton, Leibnitz, Kant, Reid, and Hamilton were famous in those countries as great scholars. As reformers of politics and religion, Pym, Hampden, Pitt, Fox, Burke, Johnson, Wycliffe, Luther, Calvin, and John Knox were noted. By these universities all science and philosophy have been improved and advanced; by them feudalism and despotism have been destroyed; by them the social ranks and the powers of the nobles and priests have been resisted; by them the desire for liberty and the demand for self-government have been awakened. The English Revolution and the religious Reformation have occurred, which have completely changed the condition of Europe. In the year 1800 there were over 100 universities in Europe. That the civilization of Europe has been rapidly advanced by the universities is a most patent fact.

"Now look at the American universities and colleges, which number over 300, and of which only 8 have been built by the government. Harvard, Yale, Princeton, Amherst, Williams, Dartmouth, and Oberlin are noted, especially the first, which is the most famous one; in it are now 110 professors and a library containing 134,000 volumes, and its endowment amounts to $14,854,372. In 1872 there were in the United States 298 colleges and universities, but during the seven years to 1879, 66 were added. This great growth of higher education in the United States is a very wonderful thing in the world.

"In the year 1620 the Pilgrim fathers landed in Plymouth; they came that they might enjoy freedom to worship God. They established a school which was founded upon Christian morality. Since that time, during two hundred and sixty years, their descendants have inherited the spirit and carried out the purpose of the fathers; they have believed that such schools would diminish the number of evil-doers and increase the number of those who do good; that they would encourage the spirit of liberty and become the foundation of the state; they have believed that in order to become a nation with the best free government they must have universities which are founded upon Christian morality, where the sciences will be taught. We cannot doubt but that their free institutions have been the result of this spirit.

"As soon as our government saw the importance of the university it established one in Tokyo, and it has also built several academies. From these we shall see some intellectual development and external advancement, but not moral development and internal improvement.

"Some are trying to improve the morality of the people; but they demand that the old morality of China shall be used with the people, and hence we cannot rejoice at their efforts, for the Chinese morality has not influence upon the mind of men generally. All Oriental states are almost destitute of liberty and Christian morality; they cannot, therefore, rapidly advance in civilization. The growth of liberty, the development of science, the advancement of politics, and the power of morality have brought forth the European civilization. These four important effects have come from the study of the advancing sciences upon the foundation of Christian morality.

"We cannot believe, then, that without morality and science civilization can come in Japan. To put the foundation of our state upon this foundation is just like putting the foundation of a building upon a rock. No sword can conquer it; no tempest can break it; no waves can overcome it. If it is put upon the old Chinese morality it will be just like putting it upon a sandy beach of the sea; when the rough waves beat against it it falls into ruin. We are, therefore, hoping for a university which is founded upon pure morality, and which teaches modern advanced science. We have been very earnest in this matter. In the eighth year of Meiji we established the Doshisha school in Kyoto, and its purpose was to teach European science and to give also moral education. Its students have increased year by year. But our aim has ever been to build a university.

"In April of the sixteenth year of Meiji we publicly expressed our purpose and received much encouragement; at this time we met our friends in Kyoto and named it the Meiji University. We have determined to raise an endowment first for a department of history, philosophy, politics, and economics, and gradually to found one also of law and of medicine. But it is not easy to establish this, for we must, as a first step, get a large amount of money with which we can erect some buildings and call some professors. We, being so few in number, cannot furnish this money, but we cannot give up our purpose to establish this university now. We must work for new Japan. All true patriots should do this. Please help us, as far as you are able, to accomplish our purpose and do this work. Unless we receive your help we cannot succeed in this great purpose."

In the early part of 1884 it became evident that the strain of the last nine years had so exhausted Mr. Neesima that he must have a complete change. He had tried in vain to rest in Japan; he could not escape from the many calls which pressed upon him everywhere; he could not forget the great work he had undertaken; it was always before his eyes and upon his heart. He at last yielded to the earnest solicitations of his friends, and accepted Mr. Hardy's generous invitation to go to the United States by way of Europe, and on the 6th of April, 1884, he started from Kobe on his long journey. He landed in Italy at Naples.

His daily journals, from the time of leaving Japan until he left Switzerland, are very full; they are little encyclopedias of information on every subject; it is wonderful to see how much information he gathered, and especially are they very full on the educational side. He visited all the schools and colleges he could, and minutely inspected their whole plan of teaching, studies, and buildings, and wrote out all the details. He secured letters of introduction to the men who were at the head of the Catholic colleges in Italy, and inspected them very carefully; also the Waldensian theological school in Florence. He spent several weeks in the Waldensian valley, and carefully studied the history, the persecutions, the school system, and the ways of working of that church. From there he went by the St. Gotthard route into Switzerland; his note-books are full of his pencil-drawings to illustrate the architecture and the processes of grape-raising, cheese-making, etc.

On the 6th of August he started with a German traveler to go up the St. Gotthard Pass. It was a gentle climb of about two thousand feet. He says in his note-book: "One and a half miles this side of the pass I began to breathe hard; I could not go; I was left behind; I stopped every ten rods; finally I reached the pass; I ate dinner, but after that I found myself worse and worse; I could not go any farther. I stayed at the Hotel Prosa until the next day; that afternoon I found myself very miserable. I thought it might possibly be the end of my life in this world. While I had a most distressed feeling in my chest I wrote my will, as follows: first paper: 'I am a native of Japan, and am a missionary to my native land. On account of my ill health I was obliged to leave my country for health. I came from Milan to Andermatt yesterday, and took a room at the Hotel Oberalp. I took a trip to the St. Gotthard Pass with a German gentleman this morning; as I found myself too unwell to go on he left me here and went on to Airolo. I found myself hard of breathing—it must be some trouble in my heart. My goods are left in the Hotel Oberalp with some money. If I die here please send a telegram to Pastor Jurino, 51 Via Torino, Milan, and ask him to take charge of my body. May the kind Heavenly Father receive my soul to his bosom. August 6, 1884. J. H. NEESIMA. Whoever reads this writing, pray for Japan, my dear native land.'

"Second paper: 'I would ask Pastor Jurino to bury me in Milan and send this writing to Hon. Alpheus Hardy, 4 Joy Street, Boston, Mass., U. S. A., as he and his wife have been my benefactors these twenty years. May the Lord give them ample rewards! Send a telegram to him at once. Please cut a little portion of my hair and send to my dear wife in Kyoto, Japan, as a token of the inseparable bond of union in Christ. My plan for Japan will be defeated; but thanks be to the Lord that he has already done so much for us! I trust he will yet do a wonderful work there. May the Lord raise up many true Christians and noble patriots for my dear fatherland! Amen and amen.'

"At this moment all sorts of thoughts came up themselves at once. I reviewed the past as well as the future. My plan for our school; my plan for a medical school; my hope to get something for these plans; my filial feeling toward my aged parents; my tender sympathy with my wife; disappointments of my intimate friends in Japan; my most grateful feeling toward Mr. and Mrs. Hardy—all these feelings and thoughts came up within me, and I struggled with them; but I can safely state here that I overcame all these feelings, and prayed to God to let his will be done in me; asked for his forgiving grace through Christ Jesus."

He gradually rallied, so that the next day he was moved in a carriage back to Andermatt; and when he was able he went on to Lucerne and consulted a physician, who told him that his heart was affected, and that he must avoid all violent exercise.

He writes from Lucerne: "Since then I feel more and more my life is not for me. Whether I live or die I must live or die for Christ. May the Lord ever keep this sin-wounded soul under his protecting hand, and count me as a least one in his kingdom, through the righteousness of Jesus Christ."

Mr. Neesima traveled leisurely down the Rhine, through Holland, and across to England, and reached the United States in the early autumn.

He attended the meeting of the Board at Columbus, Ohio, a month later, but he was unable to speak, except a few words. He rested through the winter, passing some time at the health-retreat at Clifton Springs, N. Y. He wrote a long letter from that retreat in January, 1885, urging upon us the consideration of plans for a medical

SCIENCE HALL, DOSHISHA UNIVERSITY

school, and for enlarging the evangelistic work from Kiushu and Kochi to Sendai and the Hokkaido. He says in this letter, speaking of plans for the improvement of the school: "Will you try to get choice library on all subjects? Please get up a tolerably good astronomical observatory, also good chemical laboratory; get a good supply of physical apparatus. Try to get specimens of natural history, of mineralogy, geology, etc.; try to get hold of students and hold them." At the close he says: "I am improving now; still I am sleepless and nervous too. But I can't be free from thoughts of Japan. I am a prisoner of Japan." He wrote from Boston in March, 1885: "Since February 3d I have been obliged to lay aside all my reading and writing." This brief letter was written with a trembling hand. He says: "I am still troubled with a burning headache, and have been obliged to keep myself quiet so far as I can." "I came through this winter without a serious attack of rheumatism, and the only trouble I have now is a burning, heavy headache, with occasional repetitions of pain in my forehead. I can't do much yet, but I am not discouraged; I am cheerful and hopeful."

In April and May he made a visit to Washington, stopping in Delaware and other places; but as his health improved a little his soul was wholly absorbed in thoughts and plans for his beloved land. He tried to work for the best interests of the Christian paper in Tokyo; he suggested a revision of the theological course of study in the Doshisha, to make it more scholarly; he writes from Boston, March 25, 1885: "The Board are thinking to send a graduate of Ann Arbor University to teach philosophy, etc., to make the theological department more attractive to our ambitious students. I hope your mission will heartily respond to this new movement on this side of the Pacific.

"I am glad to learn that the work in the Annaka region is so hopeful. They have recently built two more houses of worship." "It may be desirable to occupy a few important centers in Kiushu and in northern Japan, but the most important work to carry out Christ's kingdom is to raise *men after God's own heart. If you raise up strong and truly pious men to work for Christ, Japan will be ours in his name. Let us unite ourselves in this case, and push it through.* I will soon ask a lady in Louisville, Ky., to send me sixty dollars to help our needy students."

He was also working to secure a way by which Professor Shimomura could go to the United States to study, and still further to find some plan by which other men could have the foreign training they needed to fit them to teach in the Doshisha. He says in the same letter, May 26th: "With regard to founding special scholarship chairs in our school, it may be hard to raise fund enough here to secure a few American professorships, so I will work to secure the fund in Japan and raise up the native professorships. In order to do that, a few best students out of our graduates ought to be sent here to pursue the special studies to fit themselves for this new enterprise. I am strongly convinced that we can't keep up our reputation in future unless we provide a few professional studies besides theology, so I am hoping to secure a few scholarships to help our students to attain the high education in this country. We may meet many objections here and at home, but I feel we are rather compelled to take this bold step. If we could get a few scholarships here to educate and fit our students to be professors, we could start a few new chairs on political science, philosophy, history, etc., without a great expense to us. The government is doing this in the Tokyo University; why cannot we do the same in our school? I hope our friends in Japan will raise money enough for us to start this new enterprise.

"To sum up my view, let me briefly state as follows: 1. Give our students a thorough English course. 2. Make the theological course more attractive to our ambitious students. Let the foreign professors devote their time and strength for instructing this important class. 3. Provide for other professional studies to keep those boys who will not become preachers within the sacred walls of our school. 4. If I secure a few scholarships I should like to use them exclusively for the best students, intellectually and spiritually, among the theological graduates. This provision will certainly make the theological class honorable and attractive in our school. Under this fourth heading I should say still further: I called on President Porter the other day, and asked him of his view on my new plan to secure a few scholarships here. He favors this idea very much. I have been working quite hard to secure some favor for our students, very few in number, in the Johns Hopkins University, and also at Yale and Amherst. I hope they will show some special favor to our students if we send them our best specimens.

"Before I close my letter allow me to state to you that in all these my attempts I forget myself; I still suffer in my head; I feel that I am moving onward in our battlefield just as you do, though I am sent here to rest. I cannot write such a letter without shedding many tears. My heart is constantly burning like a volcanic fire for my dearly beloved Japan. Pray for me that I may rest in the Lord."

Before he returned to Japan, Mr. Neesima wrote "An Appeal for Advanced Christian Education in Japan," which was circulated in the United States, extracts from which are here given:

"Old Japan is defeated. New Japan has won its victory. The old Asiatic system is silently passing away, and the new European ideas so recently transplanted there are growing vigorously and luxuriantly. Within the past twenty years Japan has undergone a vast change, and is now so advanced that it will be impossible for her to fall back to her former position. She has shaken off her old robe. She is ready to adopt something better. The daily press, so copiously scattered throughout the empire, is constantly creating among its readers some fresh desire and appetite for the new change. Her leading minds will no longer bear with the old form of despotic feudalism, neither be contented with the worn-out doctrines of Asiatic morals and religions. They cried out for a constitution a few years ago, and have already obtained a promise from the emperor to have it given them in the year 1890. The pagan religions seem to their inquiring mind mere relics of the old superstition.

"The compulsory education lately carried out in the common schools, amounting in number to almost thirty thousand, is proved to be a mighty factor to quicken and elevate the intelligence of the masses. The Imperial University at Tokyo is sending out men of high culture by the hundred every year, to take some responsible positions either in the governmental service or private capacities. Another university will soon be founded by the government at Osaka, the second important commercial city of the empire, to accommodate the youths so anxiously craving the higher education. It will be out of the way for me to dwell here upon the material progress Japan has so recently made. But let it suffice to state that the waters of her coasts are busily plowed by her own steamers. Public roads are constantly improved. Tunnels are being cut here and there, and railways are being laid to connect important commercial points. Telegraph-wires are stretched throughout the whole length and breadth of the empire. Surveying what she has accomplished within so short a period, we cannot help thinking that she is bound to adopt the form of European civilization, and will never cease until she be crowned with success in accomplishing her national aim.

"In order to bring about the recent change and progress she has painfully sacrificed her precious blood as well as her vast treasure. Indeed, her victory has been dearly purchased. It was a quick work and was well done. It was a sudden movement, but to our great wonder very few mistakes have been made in her past course. She has tried her best as far as her capacity would allow. The most serious period of our political revolution is nearly passed, and society as well as the government will soon precipitate into some new shape. But what shape? To the writer of this article our immediate future seems a more serious problem than the past. It will be a grand achievement if a free constitution and higher education be secured to her people. But these two factors may be proved to be the very elements apt to bring out freedom of opinions, and hence the terrible battles of free opinions. A fearful national chaos might be her fate if nothing intervene to prevent it. If the nation be allowed to take her own course as she does now, hope for her regeneration might forever be gone. But in the time of need, Providence, which rules the nations with infinite wisdom, has stepped in to save us from this national calamity and despair. It was neither too soon nor too late when the missionaries of the cross from America landed on our shore to proclaim the soul-saving Gospel to the people. Through their earnest labor and constant prayers the foundation of the Christian church was soon laid.

"We believe Christianity is intended to benefit mankind at large. Why should we not undertake to extend our influence toward the higher sphere as well as toward the lower, that we might win all men to Christ? Why should we seriously object to raise up Christian statesmen, Christian lawyers, Christian editors, and Christian merchants, as well as Christian preachers and teachers, within the walls of our Christian institutions? It is our humble purpose to save Japan through Christianity.

"There might be some undue fear that such a provision of those higher studies would naturally draw away ambitious students from the theological course. It may be, but we trust we shall receive a larger supply of students in the academical course, so that some could be spared for other studies without much loss to the theological department. On the contrary, we may possibly attract some students to it from the other courses. Some evil may arise in such an undertaking, but it may be overbalanced by the good accomplished by it. Now allow us to state a few reasons for this undertaking:

"1. Such a provision will detain the youths for further studies in the school after finishing the academical course. It will help them to develop and strengthen their Christian character.

"2. Such a provision will accommodate some thoughtful parents, who may naturally desire to send their boys to a school where their moral character is carefully fostered and will be likely to be so developed as to be a safeguard against youthful vices and corruption.

"3. The youths who have thus received a broad culture will certainly have a grand opportunity to influence society for good. Words and deeds of well-educated, earnest Christians in different spheres of society will help the cause very much either directly or indirectly. Sometimes indirect efforts produce more speedy results than direct.

"4. This provision will surely benefit and tone up the

theological course, instead of causing any serious harm to it.

"5. We desire to lay down a broad basis for Christian education by encouraging post-graduate studies.

"The time is just ripening for us to take this step so as to attract thereto the best and most talented youths in the country, and foster and fit them for the highest good and noblest purpose. We are thus compelled to attempt this broad sweep to reach and win thirty-seven million precious souls to Christ. Seeds of truth must be sown now. Undue delay will give a grand chance to unbelieving hands to make thorough mischief and render that beautiful island empire hopelessly barren and fruitless. O Japan, thou the fairest of Asia! 'If I forget thee, let my right hand forget her cunning, and let my tongue cleave to the roof of my mouth.'

"But our friends are very few. The people are pressed hard on account of the business stagnation, and a most destructive flood has lately visited the country. So we cannot expect to receive from them any large donation. When we met a number of the eminent citizens of Kyoto last year for this specific purpose, we urged them to give us a fund before the year 1890, so that when the emperor gives us a constitution we might found a university to commemorate the most extraordinary period of our political history. This appeal created among them a great enthusiasm. Some of them gave us their hearty pledge to do their share. So we may possibly realize some gift just sufficient to support a few native professors. But it is beyond our expectation to receive a fund large enough to sustain even a few American professors. So if a few professorships should be given by some American friends to found chairs of political science, history, literature, philosophy, etc., it will help the cause grandly. Some people in this country may hardly realize how dangerously our shores are visited and washed by the strong tide of modern European unbelief. But to a native of the country who has been seriously watching and observing the course recently taken by the people, the present time seems grave. The future battle in Japan may not be with any foreign invaders; but it will certainly be between Christianity and unbelief.

"It is the time for us to make an extraordinary effort to push evangelical work as well as Christian education in Japan, in order to save her from corruption and unbelief. The American Board has done for us in the educational line as much as it can wisely do. Yet there remains much to be done in order to carry out our work more efficiently. The Lord's army must not be hampered while the battle is fairly commencing. Large means must be provided in order to furnish to the field strong men from time to time.

"Now who will step forth in this grand republic of America to render us timely help to save us from this impending national calamity? Here may be some friends seriously considering how their property might be best disposed of for benefiting poor humanity. With such we would earnestly plead and loudly cry, 'Remember us!' Would that God might touch the hearts of some individuals to give us a portion of their blessings, and establish chairs for advanced Christian education there as a perpetual monument of peace between the United States of America and Japan, through which the millions of our people and their posterity might be blessed!"

In the autumn of 1885 Mr. Neesima returned to Japan, somewhat improved in health, but still suffering from weakness and headache. He at once began to work

CLARK THEOLOGICAL HALL, DOSHISHA UNIVERSITY

quietly here for the establishment of the university. He made many earnest friends for the enterprise, and many sums of money were promised toward its endowment. This quiet work, and the issue and circulation of small circulars in regard to the university, continued during two or three years, but it was not until 1888 that a public and determined effort was made for the endowment of the university. About six hundred and fifty of the officials, scholars, and leading business men of Kyoto assembled in one of the large temples in Kyoto, and were addressed by Mr. Neesima and others; and much interest was aroused in behalf of the Doshisha University.

In the summer of that year Mr. Neesima went to Tokyo and worked in the interest of the university. But so great was his weakness that one evening, as he met a few friends to present his plan of the university, he fainted quite away. In July of that year, however, Count Inouye, late Minister of Foreign Affairs, gave a dinner to men of rank and wealth, inviting Mr. Neesima to be present; and after dinner he introduced the subject and asked Mr. Neesima to speak of the university, and the result was that Count Inouye subscribed one thousand yen, Count Okuma, one thousand yen, Viscount Aoki, then Vice-minister of State, five hundred yen, a prominent banker six thousand yen, and others enough to bring the amount up to thirty-one thousand yen. This gave great enthusiasm to the movement.

When the tenth anniversary of the founding of the school was celebrated, in 1885, the governor of the Kyoto-Fu, the governor of the Shiga Ken, and many other officials were present, and were greatly interested. Count Inouye had also visited the school and addressed the teachers and scholars, assembled in the chapel. It was not from any blind impulse that this money was given;

the school had proved its right to be, and that it was a needed power in Japan.

In the last English letter which Mr. Neesima wrote, only a few days before his death, from which a long quotation has already been made, he says: "Since 1884 I began to hope for founding a Christian university; the matter seemed to myself and also to my friends here that I was hoping for something altogether beyond hope; however, I had a strong conviction that God would help us to found it in his own name's sake. In order to engage in such an undertaking one shall need a strong physique; alas! my health has been poor for some years. When I made a speech before a select audience of six hundred and fifty at Kyoto, in a large Buddhist temple, in behalf of the new university, I had hardly strength enough to do it. The chief trouble was in my heart—a heart-disease. I was obliged to confine myself for some time. As soon as I became comfortable enough I attempted to move around again. In a single evening thirty-one thousand yen were subscribed, a most memorable evening to us; it took place in the latter part of July, 1888. Since then subscriptions came from the different parts of the country. At present we have raised over sixty thousand yen. We are now attempting to raise it to one hundred thousand yen before this coming summer. Since October I have been away from home, moving round here and there, though I make Tokyo the headquarters of my present movement.

"In the latter part of November I became seriously ill; I have not yet fully recovered my strength, and am now obliged to rest at a quiet country town to regain certain strength to attempt further beggings. *It is a faith work.* I have a full hope that my vague day-dream for a Christian university will sooner or later be realized, and that in some future we shall find a grand occasion to give thanks to Him who has led us and blessed us beyond our expectation. Please remember me to your Sabbath-school friends, and ask them to pray for our country."

In this connection we should speak of an appeal for the university which Mr. Neesima prepared in the autumn of 1888, and which was published simultaneously, on the 10th of November of that year, in twenty of the leading papers of Japan.

Early in August, 1888, after the money mentioned above had been secured for the university, Mr. Neesima became so weak that some physicians in Tokyo told him he had only a short time to live; one other physician told him that if he took complete rest for two years he might possibly live on several years. He went to Ikao—a health-resort in Joshu, on a mountain-side—rented a small cottage, and spent nearly two months there. He was so weak when he went up there that he was unable to ride in a jinrikisha, and was carried up in a kago or bamboo chair. When the writer visited him in that place in September, he had just become able to walk out a few rods. His stay there helped him to a little strength, and in October he returned home, but soon went to Kobe, where he could have more complete rest. He spent most of the winter in Kobe, in great weakness.

Early in the year 1887 a plan of union between the Congregational and the Presbyterian churches in Japan was proposed. Mr. Neesima was consulted but very little in regard to this plan beforehand, probably on account of his ill health; but when a copy of the proposed basis of union came into his hands he was greatly troubled. When he came to talk with me about it he was more excited than I had ever seen him before, and more troubled than I had seen him for many years.

Mr. Neesima had become greatly impressed during his

residence in America with the value of freedom; he felt that Japan needed freedom, and that it could come most safely only gradually and among those institutions which, like the Christian churches, were under the influence of men of strong moral convictions. He wanted to retain the leavening influence of the Congregational system. Differing with the experienced pastors, his former pupils, who had assisted in preparing the basis of union, he felt that the plan proposed by the committee sacrificed that principle of freedom too much, and hence he said that he must oppose it; he feared the effect of his opposition upon the Doshisha, but he said he could not yield this principle, even at the risk of severing his connection with the Doshisha and with the Kumi-ai churches. He even suggested that if the union were perfected on the basis first proposed, he might leave this part of the country and go to the Hokkaido, and work alone. I encouraged him to patiently wait and see if the proposed basis could not be modified.

In the following months, although some of his best friends told him he would ruin his hopes for a university by his course, he maintained his position, that unless the proposed basis was materially modified he could not favor it. This was a very great strain upon him during many months—a strain which, in his weakness, he could ill afford to bear.

With the spring of 1889 Mr. Neesima seemed to regain his strength in some measure; he spent some time during the summer at a seaside resort, quietly resting; and he was there when the news came to him that his alma mater, Amherst College, had conferred upon him the degree of LL.D. He wrote at this time a very characteristic letter to a member of our mission. He said that he was greatly troubled because they had conferred upon him this degree.

He had always refused any position which had been offered him in his own country, and he felt he was not worthy of this title, and he ends by asking, "What shall I do with it?"

The Doshisha had been growing all these years; the girls' school had increased its buildings and more than doubled its numbers; the training-school for nurses had been established; a preparatory department had been added to the school for young men; the first two dormitories had increased to thirteen; a large recitation hall, a chapel to seat six hundred, and a large library building had been erected, the three latter all of brick. A gentleman in New England, Mr. J. Harris, had gradually become interested in the work of the Doshisha, and had written that he was glad to take into consideration a plan to do something for the school; and this resulted first in his giving fifteen thousand dollars for a science hall, and during 1889 his interest developed into his making his gift one hundred thousand dollars to endow the science department. Mr. Neesima saw the foundations of this new hall laid before he went to Tokyo in October, 1889. The students had also increased, so that during the school year of 1888–89 there were in all departments over nine hundred young men and women.

# VI
## LAST DAYS, DEATH, AND BURIAL

*"For I am already being offered, and the time of my departure is come. I have fought the good fight, I have finished the course, I have kept the faith: henceforth there is laid up for me the crown of righteousness, which the Lord, the righteous judge, shall give to me at that day: and not only to me, but also to all them that have loved his appearing."*
—2 TIM. IV. 6–8.

*"So live that when thy summons comes to join
The innumerable caravan that moves
To that mysterious realm, where each shall take
His chamber in the silent halls of death,
Thou go not like the quarry slave at night,
Scourged to his dungeon, but, sustained and soothed
By an unfaltering trust, approach thy grave
Like one who wraps the drapery of his couch
About him, and lies down to pleasant dreams."*
                                    BRYANT.

*"Having won by toil and pain,
Who shall regret the pangs of life?
Who would regret the past's long night,
With all its fear and chill and blight,
If now the East, through twilight gray,
Were streaked with everlasting day?"*

*"The things o'er which we grieved, with lashes wet,
Will flash before us out of life's dark night,
As stars shine most in deeper tints of blue."*

*"So let the eyes that fail on earth
On thy eternal hills look forth,
And in thy beckoning angels know
The dear ones whom we loved below."*
                                    WHITTIER.

*"He does well who does his best;
Is he weary? Let him rest!
Brothers! I have done my best,
I am weary—let me rest."*

*"Say not good-night,
But in some brighter clime,
Bid me good-morning."*

## CHAPTER VI

### LAST DAYS, DEATH, AND BURIAL

THE autumn of 1889 found Dr. Neesima far from well, but yet able to be doing some work. He expressed a great desire to go to Tokyo and work for the university. His physician told him that he felt it would be better for his health not to go at all, but if he was not absent more than three weeks it might not do him any harm. He went to Tokyo in October, and saw a great many friends in that vicinity, talking of the university endowment, and receiving many promises of aid. He also visited Joshu, and while there he caught a severe cold, which confined him to his bed for a week, and left him so weak that he finally determined to go to Oiso, a quiet place on the sea-shore near Yokohama, and rest. He went there in December, and took a room in a common Japanese hotel. He was accompanied only by his clerk. Mrs. Neesima had intended to go and spend some time with him there, but his mother was taken ill in Kyoto, and as she was eighty-four years of age it seemed unwise to leave her.

The new year came, and Dr. Neesima sent out many New Year's letters to his friends, and especially to the leading pastors and workers; in one of these he said that the greatest need of the church in Japan for the new year was a *new baptism*, so that we might be prepared to take Japan for Christ. He sent an acting pastor in Niigata a letter nearly three yards long, urging upon him the importance of planting workers in the important centers of that province; he sent another long letter to a man in the extreme west end of the empire, urging the planting of the Gospel in that region.

Professors Kanamori and Shimomura spent the night of January 10th with him, and they talked over various plans for the university, the school of science, etc., and Mr. Neesima seemed as well as usual.

January 11th he began to decline, and he grew worse from day to day, so that on the 17th one of the best Japanese physicians in Tokyo was summoned to see him. He pronounced his disease peritonitis, and said that he was in a very dangerous condition. His clerk, who was with him, wanted to telegraph immediately for Mrs. Neesima, but Dr. Neesima said, "No, wait a little." On the morning of the 19th Mrs. Neesima was sent for by telegraph, and she arrived on the evening of the 20th. Mr. Kosaki, Mr. Tokudomi, and other friends had already reached his side from Tokyo.

The first word which came to Doshisha was given to the school on Tuesday morning, January 20th, and Mr. Kanamori, the acting principal of the school, started that day for Oiso. The word given to the school was "Kitoku"—"Very dangerously ill." Little circles of men were praying for the life of him they loved all that day in the school, and in the evening a general prayer-meeting was held in the chapel to pray for him; the telegrams came, in the same word—"Kitoku." That prayer-meeting was the most touching meeting I ever attended. Such tearful pleading with God I never heard before; some of the prayers were almost demands, but most of them contained the "If it be thy will."

The next day no better news came, and the praying went on, and others of the teachers and students started

NEW CHAPEL, FIRST DORMITORIES  OLD CHAPEL.

for Oiso; Thursday morning came the telegram, "No hope," then a little later, "A little hope now;" and at a quarter to 5 P.M., just as the teachers were assembling for their faculty meeting, the word was passed around of his death. No business was done but to appoint a committee to arrange in regard to the funeral, and recitations were suspended until after the funeral.

Dr. Berry reached his side three hours before the end came. He was conscious to the last, and was able to talk some up to within a few hours of his death. While he was yet able to converse pretty freely he had dictated his last words to his friends in regard to the school and to the missionary society. As he came to the last words about mission work, he had a map of five provinces spread out before him. He called for colors with which to mark, and they brought a saucer with colors on it to his bedside. With these he marked out on the map the strategic points which should be soonest occupied. As he did this he became so excited and animated over it that his friends had to check him. He asked that his wife and all his friends might come in, and he bade each one an affectionate farewell. From that time on he spoke very few words; everything was done and said that he wished to say; his soul was at rest.

A mattress and bedding had been secured for him a day or two before his death, but he said that he came into the world in confusion, and he was not worthy to die so comfortably. The last passage of Scripture which he asked to have read to him a few hours before his death was the third chapter of the Epistle to the Ephesians. This was read; friends prayed with and for him, and he gradually sank; and at about twenty minutes past two o'clock, Thursday afternoon, January 23, 1890, with the words, "Peace, joy, heaven," on his lips, he entered into rest.

Less than a month before, in a mountain village in one of the provinces, a band of children were going about the streets, their cheeks rosy with the cold. To a traveler who asked them what they were doing they answered, with sweet smiles, "We are paying Christmas visits to our friends and relatives, gathering presents; and when Mr. Neesima comes we shall give them to him for the university." Dearly beloved children! he for whom you so eagerly waited will come no more.

The following is a free translation of a poem Dr. Neesima wrote as he entered upon the new year—words almost prophetic of the end which was so near:

> "Seeing the old year go,
> Do not lament over the sick body;
> For the cock's crow is the harbinger
> Of happy times at hand.
>
> "Although inferior in ability,
> Poor in plans for the good of my generation,
> Yet, still cherishing the greatest hope,
> I welcome the spring."

Among his last words to Mrs. Neesima he said: "Do not erect a monument after my death. It is sufficient to have a wooden post stating on it, 'The grave of Joseph Neesima.'" In accordance with this request, only an unhewn stone tablet marks his grave, on which are the words, "Joseph Hardy Neesima."

Among the farewell words penned at his side just before he died are the following. To Mrs. Hardy: "I am going away; a thousand thanks for your love and kindness to me during the many years of the past, and also for the fine presents you sent me lately. I cannot write myself; I leave this world with a heart full of gratitude for all you have done for my happiness." To Dr. Clark:

"I want to thank you most sincerely for your confidence in me and in all I have undertaken. I have been able to do so little, owing to the delicate condition of my health."

The following are free translations of others of his farewell words. In regard to the Doshisha: "The future object of the Doshisha is for the advancement of Christianity, literature, and political science, and for the furtherance of all education. These are all to be pursued together as helping each other. The object of the education of the Doshisha is not theology, literature, or political science in themselves alone, but that through this education men of great and living power who love true freedom may be trained up—men who shall live for their country." "The trustees should deal wisely and kindly with the students. Strong-minded and bold students should not be hardly dealt with, but dealt with according to their nature, so as to develop them into strong, useful men. There is danger that as the school grows larger it will become more and more mechanical, hence this should be carefully guarded against." "The utmost care should be taken that the foreign and Japanese teachers may be united together in love, and work together without friction. I have many times stood between the two, and have had trouble. In future I ask the trustees to do the same as I have done." "I have not desired to make a single enemy, but if there are any who feel inimical toward me I ask such to forgive me, for I have not the least ill feeling in my heart toward any one." "I find no fault with Heaven, and bear no malice toward my fellow-men." "The work which has been accomplished is not mine but yours; for I have been enabled to do it only through your earnest coöperation, so that I do not regard it as my work at all; and I can only most sincerely thank all those who have so zealously worked with me." "My feelings in regard to the Doshisha are ever like this poem: 'In time of cherry blossoms in Mount Yoshino, morning by morning, my great anxiety is lest a cloud come and destroy the view.'"

By a curious coincidence Dr. Neesima was born on the 14th day of the 14th year of Tempo, and he died on the 23d day of the 23d year of Meiji. The body reached the Kyoto station, by rail from Oiso, at half-past eleven o'clock Friday evening, and the whole school was at the station to meet it. The school was formed in line of march, the preparatory students in front and the classes in order, ending with the theological classes in the rear. The preparatory students began carrying the bier, as many as could take hold of it, and they changed at each corner, so that when we had reached the house all had had a part in bearing the loved body. It was a scene never to be forgotten; a light snow was falling; snow covered the ground, melting into slush; but there were very few of the nearly seven hundred students who were not in line that night, and when we reached the gate of Dr. Neesima's house, two and a half miles distant from the station, before we entered one of the teachers made a very touching prayer, one of the petitions of which was that in all the funeral exercises we might do as our departed brother would desire.

On the Sabbath the casket was open in the house, and all the students and teachers of the Doshisha schools, and hundreds of others, viewed the face they loved. A memorial service in Japanese, three hours long, was held in the chapel in the forenoon, and one two hours long, in English, in the afternoon. The funeral was on Monday, the 27th. A large tent was extemporized by covering poles with tent-flies, in front of the college chapel; and all the seats from the chapels and recitation-rooms of the school were placed in it, so that three thousand people crowded into the tent, and about one thousand more stood outside. About fifty huge bouquets of flowers, arranged with branches of evergreen nearly five feet high, stood in line from the gate to the entrance of the chapel. The casket was covered with flowers in beautiful designs, and a large table in front was also covered with wreaths, anchors, etc. The service was simple: hymns; reading the third chapter of Ephesians, the last passage Dr. Neesima had read to him; two tender prayers; reading a brief history of his life; and Mr. Kosaki preached a short and very appropriate sermon from John xii. 24.

The funeral was attended by all the members of the schools; by the mercantile school, which marched up in a body; by about seventy graduates of the Doshisha, who had come from all parts of the empire; by hundreds of Christians from the city and hundreds from outside the city; as well as by many hundreds of others, including the governor and many officials of the Kyoto-Fu, the governor of the Shiga Ken, a delegation of Buddhist priests from Osaka, and by many members of his own and of other missions.

At half-past two o'clock, in a pouring rain, the procession formed, the students again acting as bearers; they had insisted from the first that no one outside of the school should touch anything; they assisted in digging the grave; they now bore the loved remains to their last resting-place, and carried all the fifty or more large bouquets, the banners, etc. The procession reached nearly from Imadegawa to San Jo Dori—a mile and a half; it went down Teramachi to San Jo, east from San Jo to the side of the mountain, and through the beautiful Buddhist temple grove where the body of Dr. Neesima's father rests (and where burial was refused for Dr. Neesima's body because he was the "very head-center of Christianity in Japan," as they said), and then wound up the mountain to a most beautiful spot overlooking the city and the mountains and valleys beyond. Many banners were borne in the procession, including one from Osaka, inscribed, "From the Buddhists of Osaka;" one, also, from Tokyo, on which was inscribed one of the last utterances of Dr. Neesima: "Free education, self-governing churches; these keeping equal step will bring this nation to honor." Many from the school also; among the inscriptions in English were: "Remember me," "There is a happy land," "Yet I live," "The truth shall make you free," etc. At the grave two hymns were sung, a prayer was offered, and the benediction closed the exercises.

The earnest, tried soul is at rest. He has heard the welcome "Well done, thou good and faithful servant: enter thou into the joy of thy Lord." He is in the midst of that joy, while we strive to finish the work which our loved brother began, the foundations of which he laid so well.

The great company of mourning friends who assembled from all parts of the empire at his funeral, and the hundreds of sympathetic telegrams which came from leading men, show how wide was the influence of this great commoner. Viscount Aoki, Minister of Foreign Affairs, sent a letter, saying, "I have lost a great and good friend." Count Inouye telegraphed to those at his sick-bed, "You must keep him alive." He still lives. Though dead, he still speaks to this whole nation.

# VII
# TRIBUTES AND LESSONS

"*Blessed are the dead which die in the Lord from henceforth: yea, saith the Spirit, that they may rest from their labors; for their works follow with them.*"—REV. XIV. 13.

"*Except a grain of wheat fall into the earth and die, it abideth by itself alone; but if it die, it beareth much fruit.*"—JOHN XII. 24.

"*Humility is the base of every virtue:
God keeps all his pity for the proud.*"
BAILEY.

"*Hath any wronged thee? be bravely revenged:
Slight it, and the work is begun; forgive it, and 'tis finished.*"

"*Good must ever live, and walk up and down the earth, like a living spirit, guided by the living God, to convey blessings to the children of men. It lives in humanity, in some form or other, like the subtle substance of material things, which though ever changing never perishes, but adds to the stability, the beauty, and the grandeur of the universe. The influence of the holy character also passes beyond the stars, giving joy to our angel brothers; and to our Elder Brother, Jesus Christ, who in seeing his own love to his and our God, to his neighbor and ours, reflected in his people, beholds the grand result of the travail of his soul, and is satisfied.*"—MACLEOD.

"*Some soul shall reap what we have sown in tears.*"
LAURA B. BOYCE.

"*They never quite leave us—the friends who have passed
Through the shadows of death to the sunlight above;
A thousand sweet memories are holding them fast
To the places they blessed with their presence and love.*"
M. E. SANGSTER.

"*Lives of great men all remind us
We can make our lives sublime,
And, departing, leave behind us
Footprints on the sands of time—*

"*Footprints that perhaps another,
Sailing o'er life's solemn main,
A forlorn and shipwrecked brother,
Seeing shall take heart again.*"
LONGFELLOW.

# CHAPTER VII

### TRIBUTES AND LESSONS

THE most difficult part of the writing of this sketch of our brother is the right estimate of his character. We are asked in what his greatness consisted. Although he had mental power above the average, that was not the secret of his power. Although he had fair executive ability, this was not the secret of his great success. He went to the United States and had extra advantages given him, so that he came back to Japan when there were very few among his countrymen who had similar advantages; but neither was this the great secret of his triumph. There was a deeper, a more subtle, and more important secret of his success than all these.

Before attempting to analyze his character I want to give a few extracts from tributes which were printed in Japan at the time of his death; also extracts from meditations found in his note-books written in Europe and America in 1884–85, and others from letters which he wrote during the last fifteen years of his life. These extracts could be multiplied almost indefinitely.

Seiran Onchi, a noted priest of the Shinshu sect in Tokyo, sent a telegram first, and afterward the following letter, dated Tokyo, January 25, 1890:

"*To the students and family of the late Mr. Neesima:*
"Having been informed in the newspaper of the death

of Mr. Neesima, president of your school, I am full of heartfelt grief. Since I am a believer in the faith of Buddhism, I stood opposed to him and often attacked his work with pen and mouth. But in regard to his generosity and prudence and great success in spreading the morality which he maintained, and his stirring the religious heart of our people with his zeal, I can have no doubt. I was especially impressed with this when I once called on him with my friend, Mr. Hakuju Takatsu. We had a few hours' talk with one another, and I was deeply impressed with the fact that he treated us with kindness and love, as if we were old friends. It seemed to me at that time that if I was not a believer in Buddhism I should have become his friend and accepted Christianity. All who are ministers of any religion must become as he was. This thought is deeply impressed upon my mind, and my respect for him constantly increases when I recollect my interview with him. To-day, when I hear of his death, his gentle countenance and lovely words reappear in my eyes and ears, and cause great sorrow in my heart. Moreover, according to the newspaper his age is the same as my own, and this fact deepens my feeling. Though I expressed my grief with a telegram, I send this letter to more fully express my feeling."

Count Katsu sent the following letter:

"I was surprised and pained at the news of Mr. Neesima's death which you sent me. Since he was too earnest in his plans, and in too great a hurry for the enlargement of his work, I used to advise him to be careful. Now, hearing of his death, I am in great sorrow. Since it must be very difficult to continue the great work he has begun, it is most important to be very careful and to expect that one difficulty after another will arise. To speak from my own experience hitherto in time of great danger, I believe that if we are sincere we shall not have our plans overthrown; and I have passed through these twenty years as if it were one day. Planning for the future will be very difficult, and there will occur unexpected difficulties. For the deceased master and for you I give this brief word of advice from an old man."

The four following selections are copied as published in Professor Hardy's "Life and Letters," pp. 331 ff.:

In the *Woman's Magazine* (Tokyo) Mrs. T. Sasaki gives the following account of an interview with Mr. Neesima a month before his death:

"Mr. Joseph Neesima, the pole-star of our religion, the founder of the university in Kyoto, died January 23d, in the 23d year of Meiji, at the age of forty-seven. We sorrow over his death, not only on our own account, but for the education of young Japan. He was overflowing with love, full of virtue and of the spirit of consecration. His departure on the eve of the completion of his great work is especially lamentable. His life is well known to the world, and any attempt to narrate it on the part of my unworthy pen would but mar the perfect gem. So I let that pass, wishing only to place before you some words of his which I wish thus to preserve as an incentive to my own spirit.

"About fifteen years ago, on his return from America, he preached frequently in Tokyo and Yokohama, and also delivered several lectures. He deeply impressed all who heard him, causing them to look upon him as the father of our people. I was one of his listeners, and from that time tried to see him as often as I could. Gradually his name became known, and he recently set about his plan to establish a university. I rejoiced in his undertaking, and to show my interest in it, with other sisters, gave a musical concert, the proceeds of which, a widow's mite, we forwarded to him. He sent us a letter of thanks, but we felt unworthy to receive even this from him.

"Last winter he came to Tokyo. It was on the 23d of December. I had the pleasure of a long talk with him. His face was gentle, but indicative of will. Though a man of few words, yet every one he uttered carried incalculable weight. He received me as a father receives his child, with overflowing love, yet with a delicate reserve.

"'Believing this is the best opportunity,' he said, 'I wish to ask a favor of you. There is a work to which I desire you to give yourself—an important one at this juncture. Among the reasons why there are so few great men among us, why national morality is so low, I believe the greatest to be the existing inequality in the rights of man and woman. Therefore the first thing to impress upon the minds of the young girls in our classes is the fact that they have individual rights and duties, that we may thus enlist their interest in the cause of religion. I have seen many girls who, after four or five years of study at the expense of much money and sacrifice on the part of their parents, enter married life to conduct themselves as if they had had no education. They do nothing for society. They are under the rule of their husbands. They have no opportunity to show their ability, but are condemned to things in which they have had no schooling—the kitchen and the care of children. This is deplorable. It is sad that their husbands, in the treadmill of petty conveniences, do not realize it. It may be the result of custom, but it is a hindrance to the progress of civilization. In matters of social reform woman's influence is greater than man's. Her power is indeed great. But in our country we still find conservative and obstinate-minded men who cling to the old order of things. Looking back over my own life

I find great troubles. A man whom I thought my sincere friend, and to whom I yielded my secret, turned out to be my enemy. For what I undertook, believing it to be for the best, I received sneers and hatred. There are unspeakable troubles in our path. Equally great are the trials which the women of to-day must meet. To ask you the favor of doing for this cause may be asking you to shorten your life. But we do not live for selfish ends, and you and I, being the servants of God, do the duties appointed for us. Therefore we must not be surprised at the sneers and evil tongues of the world, for we must not forget that the greater the trials we endure the greater shall be our reward. This that I now say is foolishness in the judgment of the majority; for, looking at the great men of the past, I find that all had to endure the sneers and attacks of their contemporaries, and even to sacrifice life. No wonder that Christ had to suffer the cross! He, therefore, who wishes to be a leader must be ready to sacrifice his life.

"'I add one thing more, and that is of the Christians of to-day. Being fed and clothed by God, they are just like dead matter. This is because they do not understand the words of God. Among many sad things this is the most deplorable. Even if thirty-nine millions of people become nominally Christian, this will not suffice to purify society. This should not be lightly thought of.'

"His words pierced me through. Some time had passed, so I rose to leave, promising to see him again with Miss Ushiwoda. On my going he presented me with his photograph, saying, 'I give you this that you may not forget what I have asked you to do.' Two days later I visited him with Miss Ushiwoda. Though very busy he received us, saying many things to us which I cannot speak of here, feeling my inability to express his thought rightly. But one sentence I shall not forget so long as I live. 'Let neither of you ever despair. Persevere. Dare to become reformers, yea, the renewers of this generation, and work on.' He seemed to be greatly moved as he uttered these words, and we left him in tears. His last words to us were: 'This may be the last time I shall see you, so please pray for me and for the Doshisha.' We went out of the door looking into his face, and sorrowfully gained our homes. From that time we prayed daily for his recovery, and for the university, when unexpectedly we heard the sad news of the 23d. We did not know even how to lament, it was so unexpected. It was the 23d of December when he talked with us—but thirty days between these two 23ds! Who could dream that those words were the last that he should speak to us? When I look back upon that day I recollect that his face showed traces of suffering, but he spoke to us as if he were unconscious of pain. Oh, his words! Even now, though I shut my eyes, I see his face clearly, and I can relate but little of what he said, for my feelings overwhelm me."

In the *Contemporary Review*, of which Mr. Fukuzawa, the great educator, is editor, appeared the following editorial:

"It is reported that Mr. J. H. Neesima died of heart-disease on the 23d inst., in a hotel at Oiso.

"There is nothing more lamentable in human experience. The death of Mr. Neesima is especially to be lamented as a loss to society. If we examine the state of society we see men attaching too much weight to everything official, as if there were no position of fame or honor outside of the government. This is the natural outcome of the feudal system. To be a government official is to be on the road to sure success. And because of this belief the avenues of official patronage are crowded. In educa-

NEESIMA'S RESIDENCE

tion and religion, as well as in politics and commerce, every eye is turned toward the government as the central source of prosperity. The existence of this tendency is disgraceful. Many things go to make up society, and of these government is one, but not the only one. In the lower stages of civilization extraordinary powers are vested in those who govern. Such a state of things would, however, be a blot upon this enlightened century, and those interested in educational and religious movements should aim at independence both for themselves and these enterprises. But is this the fact with us to-day? How many men are there among us who, free from selfish interests, seek the true independence of society? Now and then we hear a remark on this subject; but of what avail is it unless accompanied by individual illustration and example? It is as if a man who himself drinks to excess should preach temperance to others. Independent men make an independent society. Mr. Neesima, living in a corrupt age, was not corrupted by it. Working earnestly in the cause of education and religion, his purpose was ever single. He was indeed an example of independence. His body perished, but his name is beyond the reach of oblivion. Many of the coming generations will hear of him, to take heart and follow him. This may, perchance, be a comfort to his spirit. Learning the sad news of his death, we lament the loss to society of a true freeman, and present herewith our humble condolences."

Mr. J. Tokutomi wrote in the *Nation's Friend*, of which he is the editor, as follows:

"Lamartine tells us that, next to his blood, his tears are the most precious things a man can give. Individually we have lost him to whom we looked, as to a father and teacher, for strength and light and love—Mr. Joseph Neesima. As a society we have lost the leader of the cause of moral reformation in Japan. We have done our best to keep back our tears, but in vain. It is now no time to express our sorrow, for it cannot to-day be contained in letters and words. Nor is this the time to eulogize him, to analyze his character. . . . Not only brave men, but those soulless waves which wash the shores of Oiso seem to mourn for him. But his spirit of consecration still lives, and shall not we who enjoyed his personal teaching take courage and work on after him in this spirit?

"An elaborate eulogy, a magnificent funeral, a splendid monument—these would not please him. Far better is it for us to do our daily duty, to help forward little by little with our whole heart and life the moral regeneration of society, that our land may be the home of men and women loving liberty, truth, charity, and God. This, indeed, would be pleasing to him; and let him who admires his character and deplores his death think of these things. You, preachers, make your churches self-supporting. You, teachers, make your schools training places of character. You, students, seek for the spirit and energy of those who, loving liberty, can contribute to their country's welfare. You, editors, proclaim the truth fearlessly, to your enemies as to your friends. And you, all men, with all your soul and strength, love God, truth, each other."

On February 21, 1890, a large audience gathered at Koseikan, where the great public meetings of Tokyo are held, in commemoration of Mr. Neesima. The following is an extract from the address delivered on that occasion by Mr. II. Kato, president of the Tokyo University:

"You have assembled to-day to pay a tribute to the memory of Mr. Neesima. I have been requested to be present and to say something. I declined at first, for I never even met Mr. Neesima, and have had no relations whatever with him. I am not a believer in Jesus. Those who have already addressed you are all, I believe, his followers. I alone am not a Christian; neither am I a Buddhist. I am a man of no religion. . . . Yet, being urged to speak, I would like to make a simple statement. From what I have heard of Mr. Neesima I know very well what kind of a man he was—one greatly to be honored and respected. All who have spoken unite in ascribing to him an invincible purpose. It is this unconquerable spirit of his which I honor. I do not praise him because he was a Christian. I care not whether he believed in Jesus or not. I praise him for that steadfast spirit so essential in every sphere of religion, learning, politics, or trade. I believe this spirit a great necessity in this country, although it is, of course, everywhere important. We are a clever people. Western nations commend us in this respect, and they are doubtless right. Within twenty or thirty years we have, in virtue of this quality of smartness, appropriated much from the West. It is a good thing to be clever, but to be clever only is to lack strength. Cleverness and steadfastness of purpose rarely go hand in hand. The former is apt to taper away into shallowness and fickleness, and the fickle, shallow mind can rarely carry through to its end any great undertaking. While there are undoubted exceptions, yet I think this is our weakness, that we have not the endurance, the indefatigable spirit, of the men of the West. In the case of Mr. Neesima, however, from the very first, when he decided to go to America, to the close of his life, this invincible spirit was conspicuous. Such success as he attained cannot be brought about by mere cleverness.

"We are praised for the enormous progress we have made during the last thirty years. Many who, not long since, despised foreigners as barbarians, now almost worship them. From regarding them as beasts of the field, they have come to consider them as divine. This transformation has been wrought by the genius of cleverness, and it is well that it is so; but a more steadfast spirit would have brought about the change more gradually. . . . Foreigners criticize us for our mobility, and in itself mobility leads to no good results. . . . Without other qualities we cannot compete successfully with the West. Even if in actual hand-to-hand conflict we should conquer, in the competitions of peace we should be worsted. For the West is not only clever, but strong. . . . I do not say that we are altogether destitute of this element of strength, for if this were so the future would be hopeless. But I do say that for the young Mr. Neesima is in this respect a great example. Not only those who follow him in his religious faith, but all—merchants, statesmen, scholars—should strive to acquire his spirit. It is well to understand, in this age of the survival of the fittest, the necessity for this capacity to endure, and I earnestly desire that more men of his temper may be raised up among us."

At the same meeting, Mr. Takegoshi, editor of *The Christian*, said:

"In this large audience of the aged as well as the young, of men and women sitting shoulder to shoulder, there are doubtless atheists as well as Christians, theists, Buddhists, and materialists, and certainly many who never knew Mr. Neesima. Why have so many, unacquainted with him, assembled here with those who knew him so well? To honor his memory. And how shall we do this? Shall we honor him as president of the Doshisha? The Doshisha University is so firmly established that we need not grieve on its account. Shall we honor him, then, as a Christian? But this atheist, this materialist, and yonder Buddhist, how can they honor him for that reason? Why, then, are we here? This great assembly has gathered, I think, to commemorate Mr. Neesima as one of the great men of this century, whose extraordinary character is the common possession of the people. It is, therefore, more fitting to speak of him on this occasion as a hero than to relate the history of his work or to tell the story of his faith. And there arises first in our mind the question, What is a hero? Man is a being who worships heroes. The universe is the temple of hero-worship. The history of the thousands of years since man first inhabited the world is the history of this worship.

"Carlyle asserts that the worship of a false hero is the evidence of weakness, and that the homage paid to the true hero indicates a great people. Yet even great nations often bow down to the false and fail to notice the real hero who lives and dies in their midst. It is a great and glorious thing for a nation to recognize and appreciate its true heroes; and if the character of Mr. Neesima satisfies our ideal of greatness, his fame is the common glory of the nation. If a hero is one who can command an army, who rides among flying bullets and glittering swords, then Mr. Neesima was not one. If a hero is one whose eloquence, like a mighty wind, sweeps away all opposition, or whose fluent speech and practical tact insure success in every undertaking, he was not one. But if he is the hero whose life is a poem, a lesson which can be sung, and which is capable of stirring the enthusiasm of future generations, then Mr. Neesima may well be given that title. Does any one charge me with extravagant praise? I can say only what I believe. Often the fame of great men is larger than the reality. The shadow is greater than the body itself. So that on drawing near the reality disappoints us. For this reason great men are often compared to a picture which must be observed at a certain distance. But this is not the case with Mr. Neesima. Great as was his fame, when we approach nearer, to see and speak with him, he wins a larger respect. Those who knew him personally testify to his gentleness and meekness. But there burned within him a fire of mighty power. It is a very rare thing to see these two traits in a single individual. A merely good man is often weak-minded, while ability frequently leads to rashness and imprudence. Gentleness and force coexisted in Mr. Neesima to a rare degree.

"In one of his letters to me he wrote: 'Young man, fighting once, do not stop there. Fighting the second time, do not stop there. Do not stop even after fighting the third time. Your sword shattered, your arrows all spent, yet do not stop fighting till every bone is broken and every drop of blood is shed for the truth. Yes, if we do not fight for the truth, is not our life a useless one?' These words rouse me to action. When I read them I sit upright. Within, his spirit raged like the billowy sea, but it flowed out calm and peaceful in meek and gentle conduct. So a mighty river, foaming with a power to move mountains while in its bed, when it reaches the sea spreads tranquilly over the vast surface without a ripple. The secret of this combination of gentleness and strength was his confidence in Heaven. He intrusted all to God. He used to say, 'The grasses do not thank the spring breeze, nor the falling leaves complain of the autumn wind.' Autumn wind and spring zephyr were alike to him. He neither strove to win fame nor to avoid misfortune. If joy and pleasure came he did not refuse them; if they passed by he let them go and did not run after them. He left everything to its natural course. And thus on his death-bed he said, 'I do not complain to Heaven, nor find fault with any man.' He began by trusting in Heaven, he ended by enjoying it. What a sublime life! Nor did he, like an idle preacher, think lightly of his high calling.

When he was in Kobe for his health, being in Osaka, I went down to see him. Forgetful of his own illness, he conversed with me for a long time, asserting that the progress and prosperity of a nation at any epoch was to be measured by the number of its great men; and went on to speak of the scarcity of men devoted to the cause of humanity. After an hour's talk he was tired out, and fearing that he would injure himself by so long a conversation, I entreated him to stop. But he would not consent, and went on speaking as if perfectly well. The transformation of this self-seeking world into a realm of freedom and righteousness, where the old should help the young and the young care for the aged, in which the rich and the poor should cease to antagonize each other, where labor should have its due reward, and peace and prosperity brood over the entire community—in a word, the realization of the great possibilities of humanity—this was his constant aim. The great enterprise of his life had the same end in view. Riu Gen-Toku said, 'Cho-un is all courage.' So it has been said of Mr. Neesima, 'He was all courage, fire.' And this fire burned to bring forth a peaceful, prosperous nation. His tears, his prayers, his philanthropy, yea, his sickness even, were all devoted to his country. His was a vocation ordained by Heaven, and to build up on earth the kingdom of heaven he conceived to be his highest duty. We can readily understand now why he believed in himself and assumed so great a responsibility.

"If it be possible to combine truth and humanity, a bold spirit and a meek character, to show practically by one's conduct what Christianity is, without help from the dignitaries of the state or the powerful of this world, Mr. Neesima has done so. He was the Puritan of the nineteenth century. His life is like a poem which has the power to thrill and awaken. It is a precept to be followed. Such a character as his is indeed to be respected, and it is an honor to the nation to possess it.

"Ladies and gentlemen, Mr. Neesima is no more. As a mortal man, as the Puritan of the Orient, the leader of humanity, the man of independence, the lover of children, the teacher of the young, the friend of woman, the comforter of the old, he is no more. His body is buried, as was the body of the thief. But he still lives. He lives in the memory of his fellow-countrymen, in the cause of truth and humanity, in the grateful thought of the nation. You who commemorate him endeavor to follow in his footsteps; consecrate your energies to make this nation strong, upright, and noble. This is the best way to honor his memory."

The following meditations were written in his journal, July 24, 1884, while in the Waldensian Valley, Italy:

"There is great danger of our forming an opinion of others by looking at them in one case. We should be careful, because some are quite deficient in one thing, though they may be quite efficient in other things. There must be some defect found in a so-called perfect man. In the first place, find his temper; second, his education; third, his surroundings; fourth, his circumstances or situation in life; fifth, see how he behaves in some unusual case.

"Never criticize too soon; surely we shall misjudge him. Judge him with a Christian grace. Never be too harsh or too minute; love him as our Heavenly Father loves us. If we have love on our side then we may lose all our petty, criticizing spirit. Oh, it is a most unhappy and unhealthy thing to have too critical eyes for others! The best way will be not to judge others, as our Lord has taught. When we discover some defect in others, take it as if it were upon us, and try never to repeat it again. When we see great success among our brethren wish more success for him. Never look upon our dear brethren with envious eye. If he is good praise him, pray for him, and follow his example. I often observed that when some one heard good news of his friend some one would say, 'But he is so-and-so,' instead of rejoicing over his success. There is a weak human nature prevailing everywhere. There is a great deal of competition among educated people. Note: Be specially patient when we are sick or are feeling unhappy."

It is wonderful to see this man, who had himself come out of darkness only a few years before, while traveling in dark Italy alone, write down such meditations as fill his journals during those months. Here are others of the same date, July 24th: "SILENCE.—Silence is one of the virtues. There is much safety in silence. Wise men never talk much; as our mouth and tongue were given to use for good purposes, use them for good purposes. Vain and senseless talking often injures our reputation and cause us to lose our manhood. I often noticed uneasiness and chaff-like element in some vain, talkative men. There is something noble and secure in silence. Silence is a manly forbearance. A man of silence is a blessing to a family or to a society. Silence ought by no means to be combined with a bitter countenance, but with a cheerful countenance. Vain talking often disturbs affairs in a family or in society, but silence heals it. We can easily weigh a man of vain talk, but we could not easily measure the depth of the mind of a wisely silent man. But do not keep silence if we can by talking do much good to others or for the truth. Oh, how large a portion of our talk we spend for vain things of the world, and how little for the truth! When a word goes out of our mouth it is like spilled water on the parched soil—there is no possibility of taking it back again; what is said is said; it becomes a fact of our lives for which we must give account in the future. But, above all, let us not harbor evil thoughts, for evil thoughts are the mainspring of evil and vain talking."

Same date: "Poor creatures! we plan much and do very little. Our plans are often defeated by something." Same date: "Receive others patiently. If any one imitates a hero, let him be so; receive him well. If any brother do not behave as he ought, let us wait for some occasion to drop a kind word, so as not to offend him. Never send away a brother in Christ when he comes and seeks our friendship. Bear the evils of others for God's sake, for he bears our evils patiently. He does not correct us furiously, at once, but uses many occasions to heal us and takes many years to sanctify us. But let us by no means neglect our duty toward others. Look at the ocean, how beautiful it looks! Yet it must receive many filthy matters from the shores; it receives and purifies them. We shall be happy men if we can be like it. Be minute for ourselves in everything, but when we come to deal with others let us be careful not to offend them with a close calculation."

Same date: "Don't be Jack-at-all-trades. In passing through some country towns I notice that there are ever so many things spread and shown in shops, but when I closely examined each article I found that each kind is rather scanty. It is well for us to be widely informed on many subjects, but do not imitate these country shops— many articles, with a scanty supply of each. We ought to be well posted at least in one subject of the professional studies. It will be a rich treat to us. Success in our life will chiefly hang upon it. Let this be our offensive or defensive weapon on the battle-field of truth. Though our talent may be small, yet it is solid and weighty. *Be single-minded for a single purpose.* We shall sooner or later reach our mark. Never shoot our arrows into the air; aim at an object surely, and then let it go. If we miss, then repeat the process again and again until we can satisfy ourselves. I never knew a single case of a talented, puffed-up, yet unsettled-minded man having accomplished anything noteworthy."

Same date: "Never miss a rare occasion to do good. Let our guns be always loaded. When we meet our game, aim at it and shoot it instantly, for our game will never wait for us. When we meet any occasion to do good to others, then don't let it go. Don't wait for to-morrow; do it at once, for we may never have the occasion again. To shoot wild game is a mere pleasure, but to shoot men for our Master is a grave business. Let our guns be first loaded with living powder and bullets from on high, and be always ready. Many hunters of men carry their guns unloaded; this explains the reason why Christ's kingdom among men does not spread faster."

Same date, July 24th: "At my sick-bed. THE DIVINE FIRE.—Many Christian ministers may have highest culture, and may write their sermons with much skill and thought—beautifully executed work, like a Grecian marble statue. Alas! there is no heat in it. Heat must be caused by fire; if there is no fire in the sermon to heat the hearers' hearts it is a serious affair. This fire can only be got by daily seeking. Those who depend very much upon their talent and knowledge are very apt to forget to seek this much-needed divine fire for themselves, as well as for their hearers. How cold such a heart must be to a congregation! If each professing Christian has this divine fire Christ's kingdom will come much faster. O Heavenly Father, give us this fire! However small we may be, if we have genuine fire we shall consume even the whole world. How small a spark of fire burned up a vast forest in Canada! How small a lamp-light consumed two thirds of the great city of Chicago! Sometimes one may make an artificial fire in imitation of the divine fire, but his hearers will sooner or later detect it; it is a mock fire. God will not bless such. Oh, let the divine fire be burning within us always!"

Same date: "MAN'S GREATNESS.—Man's greatness is not simply in his learning, but in his disinterestedness in self. Those with much learning are apt to be more selfish than the unlearned. Let us look at Christ on the cross. He is our example. Oh, how noble, how grand, how gracious he seems to us! Let us forget self, and offer ourselves freely for the cause of truth and good. Let us also be truly penitent and humble. I call this man's greatness."

The above meditations were written in one day, when, after going up on a mountain excursion from Rosa in the Waldensian Valley, he says: "We passed one night in the mountain house. I sent my thick coat and shawl with a donkey, and the donkey did not come that evening. I had to go without my shawl; I slept under the hay—uncomfortable." The result was that the next day, July 22d, he had a fever, and it took him two days to get back to Rosa again. His entry for the next day after his return, July 24th, is: "I was quite unwell; called Dr. Vala; he gave me quinine once in two hours." Yet on this day, "at my sick-bed," he wrote the meditations above given.

Here follow other meditations from his journal: "A THOUGHT FOR PREACHING.—Suppose the future Judge

NEESIMA'S STUDY

of the moral world comes down now and summons each of us to appear before him, and uncovers all our past deeds before the congregation, how many of you will dare to step forward and get all your deeds eternally penned upon the walls of the sacred edifice, to be read by each of you?"

"HUMAN HAPPINESS.—God gave us a sense of happiness so that we might be truly happy. It is right for us to feel happy when anything is given us from him. Let us be happy for the daily bread we receive, happy for pleasant circumstances, good home, good friends, pleasant situation, etc. But all the earthly happiness will become as nothing at all when we are permitted to step through the gate of Paradise and catch the glory of the Lamb of God, who caused the gate of heaven to be opened to us; let us aim at this happiness; this only is abiding."

"PROMISES.—Fulfil your promises promptly; never postpone until to-morrow, for we may not see it, or may be fully occupied with something else; then we shall have no occasion for excusing ourselves for the delay. It is a sort of weakness and sham for a man to make all sorts of apologies to another; let yea be yea and nay be nay. Do or not do. Never be sluggish, and never leave business half done."

"BUSINESS CHARACTER.—The Italians appear to be polite, but they lack business character. They are easy and like to be easy. They would rather postpone their business if they can. They will not move unless they are pushed by some one. Do your business promptly when it is required to be done. Do not waste your time by talking; do it at once and it is done. Try to talk what we mean, but never talk anything which we do not really mean in our heart. It is a moral weakness to say what we do not really mean. Straightforwardness can be found mostly among the Anglo-Saxon races, English and Americans."

"Roughness and Politeness.—A rough manner with a kind heart is far more preferable than a petty politeness with no least meaning. Japan is one of the politest nations in the world, but, alas! their heart is far from it. Artificial politeness became the national habit. This is not the result of true sincerity. Politeness ought to be a necessary exponent of true love and kindness, but politeness without a least meaning is a sort of deception. Remember that we are always naked before Him who never slumbers nor sleeps."

"Watchfulness.—Watch, pray, and be prepared for the Master's call. We know not when he will come, whether in the first watch, the second watch, the third watch, or the fourth."

"A Policy for Our Training School.—Let us be like an unpolished diamond; never mind the outward rough appearance if we have a shining part within. Let these three factors be our perpetual mottos: 1. Christ as our foundation-stone. 2. Well-qualified instructors. 3. Well-selected library and thoroughly equipped apparatus. Those three factors will be true and shining parts of our training-school. Too much of brick and mortar does not suit my humble taste. I am terribly craving for the inner polish that will be a glory of our school; that will certainly command the respect of the thoughtful Japanese more than brick, stone, and mortar."

"The True Hero-worshiper.—Most of the Japanese will be hero-worshipers; they are a hard set of people to be managed, except by a hero to whom they can look up. Yet they are very easy to be led away by a hero. They are moved with the sensational currents of the hero's opinions. There is a lack of individuality in them. Most of the hero-worshipers will be always colored by the same tint as the hero himself. The weak point is that they do not rise above their hero. If the hero makes a mistake or failure in his career they will do the same. If the hero falls they will fall likewise. The matter has been so with us when we examine our history closely. You will also find that there has been no hero in Japan who has done all for unselfish ends. He is apt to be more selfish than the common mass of the people. If their mind could be directed toward the Hero of heroes, the greatest the world has ever produced, I am sure it would revolutionize the future of Japan. He is far above Socrates and Confucius, yet he is a friend of the poor. He is far above Alexander and Napoleon, yet he shed his own blood for the people, instead of shedding the blood of hundreds of thousands of innocents for his own gratification. He had no selfish aim in his life; he was perfectly holy and yet perfectly simple; he had no place to rest his head, yet he sat from eternity on the throne of the universe. If the Japanese are bound to worship heroes, let them worship this Hero, the Hero of heroes. His worshipers will also be tinted with the one best color, that is, the color of godliness. Within this bound there is an ample scope for freedom; man can choose any professions except bad and harmful ones. In following and worshiping him we shall obtain the true human liberty; we shall certainly have our individuality. Oh, how I long that our people should turn their attention to this Hero, who is far above weak humanity!"

"QUESTIONS.—Is there any one in the world who is altogether above selfish ambition? How can he know himself that he is perfectly free from that? How can we know that such an one is free from it? Is there also any one who is perfectly free from the slightest deception?

Could ever deception be eradicated from civilized society? How many of us could say to God that I have lived my life without the slightest ambition or deception? Has any one ever seen, or could we ever expect to see, such a perfect type of humanity among the race of Adam, except the Son of God? It is too foolish to entertain such a question. But I would like to meet a person of the above description."

"A BEST METHOD OF TEACHING.—If I teach again I will pay a special attention to the poorest scholar in the class; then I shall succeed."

In a letter from Tokyo, March 24, 1878, he closes as follows: "Pray for me, so that I may be directed entirely by His hand." After an absence in Tokyo, on his return he writes:

"KYOTO, Monday morning, July 21, 1879.

"I arrived in Kobe yesterday at 5 P.M., and passed the last night in Nishinomiya. I might have returned home last night, but lest I should break the Sabbath I stayed at the above-mentioned place. I came home this morning a little after nine o'clock. I have not seen Mr. Yamamoto yet, but I don't believe the present difficulty is very serious. We have the strong God to depend upon. I trust he will make the matter all right."

During the revival at the time of the Dai Shimboku-kwai, or General Conference, in Tokyo, he writes:

"TOKYO, May 11, 1883.

"DEAR BRETHREN IN KYOTO:

"I am anxious to write a few lines to inform you how the Lord blessed us in our Dai Shimbokukwai. We commenced it on Tuesday, with a one-hour prayer-meeting. It was the most impressive meeting I ever attended in my life. A spirit of union was greatly manifested in that meeting; then followed the business meeting; Mr. Miyagawa was elected chairman. In the afternoon we had reports of the delegates; it was a most enjoyable part of the conference. I can assure you that the Lord blessed us far more than we asked for."

When he had heard news affecting the Doshisha which greatly troubled him, he writes from Dorchester, Mass., March 22, 1885: "We shall be in a hard fix then. I know not what to say, but I can only state to you that *I am on my knees.* I hope I shall get a further light upon this serious subject." In the same letter he speaks of the great trials and difficulties of the past, and says, "I often wonder how I ever came through those deep muds of the past;" but he adds, "I received the sustaining courage and strength from the unseen Hand;" and again at the close of the same letter: "Recently I learned something from experience: when I meet any serious or alarming case I keep myself *standstill*—not to be frightened by them; afterward they pass off all right." Again, when serious misunderstanding had arisen in regard to Mr. Neesima's action, and a letter had been sent to him which he calls "the most insulting letter I ever received in my life," he writes from Milford, Del., in regard to it, April 20, 1885: "I am sorry to say that his letter is thrown into the wastebasket. When I read it I said within myself, 'What! have I lost a sense of honor?' but I knelt right down for God's grace to preserve me in his hand. I am all right now; please don't mention it to any one." "I thank God for his ever-sustaining grace to me. Each trial and each difficulty draws me nearer to his hand; he sustains me and helps me far beyond what I can ever know or discover. Pray for me that I may be ever nearer to him."

May 26, 1885, he closes a long letter of ten pages, written from Boston, which is full of plans for the school and for the spreading of the work in Japan, with, "Pray for me that I may rest in the Lord." When starting for Tokyo in August, 1875, to try and get permission to start the Doshisha, he closes his letter with the words, "Pray for my success."

By the advice of the mission, Mr. Neesima spent the summer of 1887 in Sapporo, on the island of Yezzo, and while there he heard the news of Mr. Hardy's serious illness, which came by cablegram to him. He writes to Mrs. Hardy: "July 30, 1887. Mr. Hardy's letter informing me of the action of the prudential committee was received here with a grateful heart. Alas! the intoxication of this joy was soon dampened by the telegram telling me of his serious illness. I had some fear of it since receiving your last letter. How greatly I am troubled I can scarcely state here. I wish we could have some sort of medium to convey our messages every hour. Oh, how anxiously I feel about him! He has sown with us, and I earnestly wish he could reap much more fruit here in Japan with us before he departs in peace. Besides, I do own a real affection for him, and think I love both of you more than my own parents. I am begotten of you by your love. Pure love kindles love of the same kind. Noble affection binds us much firmer than some natural ties. I wish I could appear before him even in his dream."

After hearing of Mr. Hardy's death he writes: "August 24th. I am all confused when I attempt to write to you. I have many things to say to you concerning Mr. Hardy's departure for another world. But when I attempt to write, alas! I find everything chaotic. I sit by my table, I hold my pen—but I can do nothing further. Of course I know that our Heavenly Father wished him to come to the blissful heaven. I know we must submit all our affairs to his hand. I know, also, Mr. Hardy may be far better off than in this troublesome world; but I miss him very much—I feel quite lonely. I feel my real father is gone; yea, he has been to me more than my father. I believe that he knew me more than all my Japanese friends here. I have lost the friend of Japan. My heart is darkened like the total eclipse which so recently happened here. Cheerfulness and brightness are suddenly disappeared. Alas, the total darkness! The air is chilled, the temperature is fallen. This solar eclipse lasted only for a while, but my heart's eclipse may last as long as I live. I cannot finish even these few lines. I am too sensitive just yet. Besides this sensitive feeling I have another—my sympathy with you. You must miss him beyond measure. His cheerful voice cannot be heard any more. My heart aches in your behalf. However, I rejoice with you that when he departed from you he must have commanded you to trust and rely upon another Arm, ever strong and everlasting. I will try and write you much oftener than before, but at present I find it a hard task to write to you."

"September 4th. It is quite rainy this afternoon. I am undisturbed by any visitor; my heart turns to Boston. My reflection about you and Mr. Hardy is taking hold of my heart very strongly. This is the fifth Sabbath since he left us, but with him it must be the continual Sabbath. We who are left behind weep and mourn, but he rejoices. All the mysteries here may be no longer any mysteries to him. How grand that must be! While I am sadly missing him, and at the same time cheered by the idea of his most holy, happy, and blessed state, I have a mixture of contrary feelings. We all feel we have lost the father of the Japan mission. Some sent me telegrams to console my sorrow, others wrote me letters to express their own. Now we have got to go on without his advice and support. At this critical hour I simply cry out, 'God help us!' I would like to write you some things I have observed in this island. At present I have no courage to do so. I have received your letter telling me of his most loving memorial to me. Now I must say what a touching thing it is that he should remember me so far away as he did. I shall never, never forget it. Through God's help I will try to follow his example. Doubtless your letter was written with many tears. So it is with mine. My heart is still burning with all sorts of plans for our work. But my wife is a constant guard to check me and take away my control. She works like a policeman to remove my pens and papers, and requests visitors to cease their conversation. I told her that I cannot hide myself anywhere in Japan now, and I am thankful for it."

After the physician had told him of the serious nature of his heart-disease, he wrote Mrs. Hardy from Tokyo, July 4, 1888:

"Allow me to send you my compliments for this glorious day of your nation. I came here on the 11th. My wife is with me. She is a sort of policeman over me, watching lest I overdo. Though I am slightly gaining, I believe I shall never get well again. My doctor says my heart is enlarged and will never resume its original size, and that at any time my bodily life may cease. Of course I bore it rather bravely, but to my wife it seemed almost unbearable. She was warned to keep it a secret from me. But, poor creature! she could not keep her secret. I tried to comfort her, and told her all my future expectation. However, I found it a hard work to quiet down my own sensitive feelings. Since then she stays with me, and does not give me a chance to write much. Just now I sent her away a few minutes in order to write this letter. Though I am absolutely prepared to resign my future into the tender hand of the Heavenly Father, yet when I think of you—all my past affairs—your motherly and unceasing love comes at once to my memory, and I weep like a babe. I dislike to pass off suddenly without a good-by to my dear friends. Therefore, though it may be useless to inform you of such a matter beforehand, I should be sorry to leave this world without sending you my last farewell, with my unspeakable thanks for all you have done for me. I owe you all, and have nothing to pay back but my thanks and daily prayers for you. If I fail to send you my last farewell by reason of passing off suddenly, as my doctor described to me, please regard this as my last word to you. I wish I could write as I feel, but I cannot express myself at all. I trust you can guess at it. What I cannot say I hope I shall say in another world. With regard to my tender feeling to my dear wife and aged mother you may sympathize with me. You know, also, how much I am interested in our Kyoto schools and the Gospel work throughout this island empire. I am willing to leave all these interests behind. I am thankful for what has been done for my beloved country. What now shall I hope or expect to receive? As you know, I have a desperate plan and will to make our Kyoto school a Christian university. For this cause I came to Tokyo. For this cause I became ill and fainted away. For this cause I am still staying here. However, I am very careful. I fear I cannot write you much hereafter. If I pass off I hope you will not feel too sorry. I fear this may not be a very complimentary letter to receive on your Fourth of July. But so long as I am prepared to resign myself to His hand, I like to tell my sympathizing mother and ask for her prayers for my soul. My wife has returned and warns me to stop. What I write here is not revealed to her. Please keep this secret from other people. I am still hopeful to live, but am prepared to go also."

The following are translations of some of the poems which Dr. Neesima wrote on different occasions. The first is one composed two days before he left Japan the first time:

"One suit of rough clothes and a sword of three feet long I have; when I turn my head and look at the affairs of the world, I feel rather depressed in my heart. Man has by nature an aspiration for a great journey. Unless I travel through the great cities of the five continents I will not take my rest."

The next was composed when he reached the China Sea after he left Japan: "If man be determined in his mind to run away a thousand miles, he expects to have to endure great sufferings, and why can he be anxious about his home? But how strange! In the night, when the spring wind is blowing, in a dream he sees flowers in the garden at home."

Here follow three poems composed on the journey when he went to America the second time:

"The feeling aroused by parting during life is stronger than that of parting in death. When we are parting from each other how can our hearts be light and jubilant? A traveler to the Western land in nightly dreams sees a school by the side of the river Kamo" (in Kyoto).

"Even an iron steamer seems to know the feeling of departure; for it moves slowly toward the West, breaking the waves. The ferry-boat which conveyed me is disappearing in the evening mist. When I look at Mount Rokko in the far north, the scene is gloomy and dark."

"For ten years I cherished the hope of a foreign trip in

vain. At length I am, to-day, outside of my native land. Flowers in Paris may be beautiful, the moon in London may be fair, but in my dreams I search after the people by the side of the Shokoku-ji." (The river Kamo is near Doshisha, and Shokoku-ji is the name of a large grove just back of the school.)

*Miscellaneous Poems.*

"The serpent-like criticism of the world I do not mind at all. For thousands of years I will lie patiently in the great marsh. Behold, when there come great winds and clouds I will fly to the top of Mount Fuji."

"Though I am sickly myself, how can I be without anxiety in my heart? With patience I expect to see success. Being diligent we must polish our spirit as a gem. The light of God does not yet shine in this land of the mikados."

"Cease to say that human affairs are all dangerous. Wherever there is justice there is the will of Heaven. If my faith be as a mustard-seed I can change the mulberry-field to the blue sea and the blue sea to the field." Here follow two poems, one composed as he was about leaving Japan the first time, and the other when he returned to Japan:

"The aspiration of a knightly man is like a maple-tree on Mount Tatsuta. He will not come back without wearing glorious clothes."

"A glorious cloth to decorate the fatherland is hidden in the box, because it is not time to wear it."

Dr. Neesima had a deep vein of humor in his nature. In June, 1875, the first time I went to Kyoto with him to look at the land for the Doshisha, we visited the San Jiu San Gen Do, a Buddhist temple, where are a thousand life-size wooden images. As we walked among them, Dr.

Neesima said with a laugh, "These images are just fit to keep poor students warm in the winter." A missionary once sent a very *cheap* kakemono, or wall picture, to a friend in America. When Dr. Neesima was in the United States the last time he visited this friend, and was shown this article, over which a great deal more ado was made than the article warranted; he was asked to explain it, and he told the missionary who sent it, after he returned to Japan, "I read all the characters except the price-mark; I thought," said he, with a twinkle of the eye, "you would be willing I should omit that." Only a day or two before he died, when his wife and one or two other friends were changing his clothes, and causing him to groan with the severe pain, "Oh, how you hurt," he said with a groan; and then added, "This is the first time I've ever been stripped by *good* people."

Dr. Neesima told one of our number the following incident of his early boyhood. His father was rather strict with him, and one day whipped him severely on his hand; this made him very angry, so that he sulked and would not speak to his father; so after a day or two his father called him to the little garden, pointed to a delicate bamboo, called the sasa, and recited this poem: "Nikunde wa utanu mono nari; sasa no yuki"—"I do not strike in anger; snow on the sasa." As snow bends and almost breaks the delicate sasa, we must tap it gently so that it will rise erect again. By this Dr. Neesima felt touched, knowing his father's love for him, and he ceased his sulks. When Dr. Neesima began the study of the Dutch language in Tokyo he needed a dictionary, but he had no money; so he opened his father's money-drawer, took out eight yen, and put in its place a paper saying he had taken it and would replace it some time; when the money was missed and the paper found Dr. Neesima said that he had bor-

FIRST CLASS IN DOSHISHA UNIVERSITY, FIFTEEN YEARS AFTER GRADUATION

rowed it, and that he had to run in debt two yen more to get the dictionary; whereupon his father gave him the balance of two yen.

Miss Isabella Bird describes her visit at Dr. Neesima's home in her "Unbeaten Tracks in Japan," vol. ii., pp. 232–235. She says: "Mr. Neesima is a gentleman to begin with, and has quiet, easy, courteous manners. He is a genial, enlightened Christian and an intensely patriotic Japanese. He gives a sad account of the lack of truth and the general corruption of morals among his countrymen. I asked him what, in his opinion, are the leading faults of his countrymen, and he replied, without a moment's hesitation, 'Lying and licentiousness.'"

Dr. Neesima was present at the opening of a branch Sabbath-school in a large pottery in the southern part of the city of Okayama in the fall of 1880, and was invited to preach the first sermon. In it he emphasized the need of being pure in heart, and told of seeing in America a beautiful and costly Japanese vase which the gentleman had recently purchased. He admired and praised the workmanship to the gentleman's satisfaction, but when asked to explain the designs he hung his head. "There," said he, "were the signs of our country's shame; the designs were too vile to be told."

Dr. Neesima's character contained the principle of love to a marked degree. He had strong love for his friends, and it was a love which was broad as well as deep. He deeply loved the students of his school, and this love was universally reciprocated by the students. He loved them so much that it almost broke his heart to have any of them leave the school on account of dissatisfaction, or to have to send any one out of the school as a punishment. He could hardly bear to exercise discipline in the school. On one occasion, during the earlier history of the school, some grave offenses had been committed, and yet Dr. Neesima felt that the school was partly to blame or such things would not happen, and instead of punishing the offending students he said the Doshisha must be punished; so one morning at prayers in the chapel he stated those convictions to the school, and said that he was going to punish the Doshisha and he could do it in no other way than by punishing the head of the school; and so, taking a stout withe in his right hand, he struck his left hand a succession of blows which brought the tears to every eye in the house before one of the older students could interfere to stop him. In all his connection with the school I never heard a student say anything against him, and I never knew that one did so.

Dr. Neesima's love for the members of his own mission, and for all the foreign workers in Japan, was very strong, and they loved him in return. His earnest yet simple and unassuming ways won all hearts and begat a love which no discussions or difference of opinion interrupted. He had the love and respect of all the foreign workers in Japan who knew him, and he had no more sincere mourners at his death than the large company of foreign friends of different missions who gathered at the memorial services in Kyoto and in other places.

Another trait was peace. He tried as much as in him lay to live in peace with all men. He was ready to yield his own view; this was almost a fault with him. He was sometimes too ready to yield to the opinions of others. During all the years of his connection with the school as its president and head, he never once, so far as I know, set up his opinion against that of the teachers; he always yielded and worked in harmony with them. He was always ready to yield any point which he felt was not contrary to the great aim of his life; when that was at stake the whole world could not move him. He was generally a joyful, cheerful man. His strong faith and hope kept him in an atmosphere of joy. So, too, we might speak of his long-suffering, gentleness, and goodness; also of his faith; in the darkest hours his faith in God and in ultimate success only seemed to grow stronger.

His meekness was remarkable. He was from the first the head of the school, and yet, during all those years, he kept himself in the background and never insisted on his rights as president. It was hard work to get him to take the president's seat on the platform in the chapel.

When, however, we go deeper and seek the mainspring of these graces, we find, as the Apostle tells us in Galatians v. 22, 23, that they were all the "fruit of the Spirit." The mainspring of Dr. Neesima's character, and the secret of his great success, was in his union to God in Christ through the Spirit. He felt, with Paul, "I can do all things through Christ who strengtheneth me."

It is difficult to analyze the great secret of his power and success, but we may mention a few points:

1. Loyalty to duty. As soon as he gained an idea of God he felt his obligation to him, and he began to discharge it; and as the months and years went on and his vision of duty broadened, his sense of obligation broadened with it, and efforts to discharge that obligation kept pace with his enlarging vision.

2. He took a great aim and one which was in harmony with God's great aim. He did not take a low aim, he did not take a selfish one; he took for his aim the establishment of a great Christian university, for the sake of lifting up, so far as he could, through that, his whole nation toward God and a Christian civilization. The results of that school are already changing the history of the empire.

3. He had a holy, absorbing ambition to realize his

great aim. He counted not his life dear to him if he could accomplish his great object. When, a few years before he died, the question was raised of his going to the United States a third time to try and secure money for the endowment of the university, and his physicians told him it would be almost certain death for him to go, he replied that that would make no difference with him if he felt that by going he could secure the money. His going to Tokyo and working during the last months of his life were done in a similar spirit. He wanted to die in the harness, and he did.

4. He committed himself and his great plan and all its details to God, with a firm faith that God would give him success. He never seemed to waver even in the darkest days. In the last English letter which he wrote this faith shines out. After speaking of the gift of $100,000 for the Scientific School, just as Professor Shimomura was ready to return to his work in the school, he says: "Is it not wonderful that when he was about ready to come home the way to make himself useful was opened before him?" And then in that letter he tells of his "day-dream to found a Christian college," and how he received no human encouragement; but he says: "However, I was not discouraged at all; I kept it within myself and prayed over it." Then the night before he made his appeal for money at Rutland he could not sleep, and says: "I was then like that poor Jacob, wrestling with God in my prayers." Then later, when he took up the larger work of founding a university, he says in the same letter: "I have a full hope that my vague day-dream for a Christian university will sooner or later be realized, and in some future we shall find occasion to give thanks to Him who has led us and blessed us beyond our expectation."

5. His heart was greatly interested in direct mission

work. Deeper than all other thoughts, more important than all other plans, was the thought and the planning to bring the millions of Japan to Christ. This was fundamental to his whole plan for a Christian college and university.

When the writer visited him for an hour in Ikao, where he rested in great weakness during the summer of 1888, he was no sooner seated than Dr. Neesima said, "I have something I want to show you;" and he went to the adjoining room and brought out a map of the province of Joshu, and on it he had marked every place where there was a church, every place where the Gospel was regularly preached, and other places for which he was praying and planning to secure evangelists. He had no greater sorrow during the closing years of his life than that which came from the fewness of those from among the graduates of the collegiate department of the Doshisha who prepared themselves to preach the Gospel directly. He was often ready to weep over it as he spoke of it, and he wept as he prayed over it.

He begins his round-the-world diary in 1885 in the following words: "April 6th. Went on board the 'Khiva' at Kobe, accompanied by my wife and other friends. I separated from my wife with prayer, committing her to the care of my Father in heaven, upon whom she can rely far better than upon myself." "April 7th, Monday. Prayer for theological students." "April 8th. Came to Nagasaki 6.30 A.M.; pray for fifth year;" and so on, day after day, we read, "Pray for vernacular class," "Pray for theological class." He carried this intense desire for workers to be raised up to reap the waiting fields of Japan around the world with him, and presented this object in earnest prayer to God every day.

He always let his Christianity be known; as has been

mentioned on previous pages, his first work when he reached his native land was to preach the Gospel to the people in his old province of Joshu; he did it so earnestly that it has brought forth an abundant harvest. His first work when he came to Kyoto, in 1875, was to start a religious service in his house on the Sabbath, where he preached Christ to a little company of men and women. Dr. Neesima was always and everywhere known as an earnest Christian; the impression of him among his countrymen was well voiced by a high official who remarked, when Dr. Neesima had persisted in holding firmly to his Christian principles, "Well, you are a *slave* of Jesus Christ, are you not?"

Dr. Neesima spent the summer months of 1885, while in the United States and far from well, at West Goldsborough, Me., a retired country place. On July 28th he wrote to Mr. and Mrs. Hardy as follows: "I went to church here last Sunday. After service I asked for the Sunday-school. To my surprise the reply was negative. I thought it too strange and too bad that these young folks should grow up here without it. A thought came to me at once, Why cannot we start a Sunday-school here? I proposed to a lady here that we should offer ourselves as teachers. I thought I would not show forth myself as the originator of the idea, and tried to put the preacher forward to execute it. He was most too glad to do so. I took the responsibility of getting the Sabbath-school papers for them, because I had no least doubt you will take a share in the work and get others interested in it."

Professor Hardy says ("Life and Letters"): "In his subsequent letters from Japan, when burdened with many cares, and feeling the hand of death not far from him, Mr. Neesima asks again and again, 'How is my Sunday-school getting along?'"

LAST RESTING PLACE

What, then, are the lessons of this life to us who remain?

1. Let us realize that still

> "God moves in a mysterious way
> His wonders to perform."

The age of miracles of physical healing may be past, but we have before us the fulfilment at the present day in the world of the Saviour's promise, "Greater works than these shall he do; because I go to my Father." The wonderful calling of Dr. Neesima twenty-six years ago; his preparation; the bringing of Captain Janes to Japan and the training of the band of men who should be associated with Dr. Neesima to make his school and his work a success; the bringing to this land of the missionaries who should be associated with him in that work; the planting of the school in Kyoto, in the midst of the great prejudice and opposition, and its success as it stands before the world to-day, is as great a miracle as any recorded in the Old Testament or the New, if we except the miracle of our Saviour's incarnation and atoning work. It is simply inconceivable that all these improbable things should happen, and that they should come together at just the right time, simply by chance.

2. Let us all grasp the fact of the greatness of the work which God used our brother to begin. When God called Abraham out of his native country to go into a strange land, he had a great purpose and work to accomplish through him. God does not work such wonderful deeds as this sketch contains without having a great plan and purpose to accomplish through them. We can see already that the Doshisha is changing the history of Japan; and if the plan of our brother can be carried out this school will be one of the greatest factors in the civil-

ization and Christianization of Japan. But if this is to be the result then all the friends of the school, foreign and Japanese, must realize the greatness of the sacred trust which they have inherited from its beloved president, and, with a similar love and faith and hope and patience, they must hold the school true to the great purpose of its founder: not education for its own sake, but education for the sake of God's glory and the salvation of men.

3. We may learn that self-denial for Christ is the greatest gain for self; that he "who would be great must be a servant: and that he who would be first must be servant of all." God takes care of the man who is loyal to him, loyal to his own conscience, loyal to duty, loyal to right. The happiness and final success and glory of that man follow of necessity, because it is a part of the eternal nature of things, and because God will sooner or later put his approving smile upon that man and upon his work. Dr. Neesima's name will be remembered on earth long after the names of many so-called heroes are forgotten, and his place in heaven will be above that of every man who has sought his own glory.

4. Let us remember that just as Dr. Neesima's life was a plan of God, so every man's life may be a plan of God. If we will but put ourselves in God's hands, to be led and used by him, and work with God and let God work with us, we shall work in harmony with God, we shall work with God, and our power and ability will be multiplied by an infinite factor, so that God only can measure, and eternity alone can reveal, the results of our life-work. "The good man does better than he knows!"

"Blessed are the dead who die in the Lord." Dr. Neesima rests from his labors, and his works follow him.

www.ingramcontent.com/pod-product-compliance
Lightning Source LLC
Chambersburg PA
CBHW032152160426
43197CB00008B/886